WITHDRAWN

# YOUR MOTHER WEARS COMBAT BOOTS

*Humorous, Harrowing and Heartwarming Stories of Military Women*

Michele Hunter Mirabile

authorHOUSE®

6/10 LAD 5/09 1 (0)

*AuthorHouse™*
*1663 Liberty Drive, Suite 200*
*Bloomington, IN 47403*
*www.authorhouse.com*
*Phone: 1-800-839-8640*

*First published by AuthorHouse 11/14/2007*

*ISBN: 978-1-4343-2044-5 (sc)*
*ISBN: 978-1-4343-2045-2 (hc)*

*Library of Congress Control Number: 2007905252*

*Printed in the United States of America*
*Bloomington, Indiana*

*This book is printed on acid-free paper.*

*"Your Mother Wears Combat Boots* offers a fascinating look into the lives of women who make up today's Total Force, while providing honest and insightful accounts of how they built on the experiences of the women before them, and set the standards for those who will follow." **Brigadier General Tom Brewer, AUS (Ret)**

*"Your Mother Wears Combat Boots* is a compilation of real stories written by real women who have served in the United States Armed Forces. These extraordinary women now share their remarkable experiences and their most private emotions while providing the reader a glimpse of the conditions that shaped them. They speak the common language of the soldier and the officer, a language that anyone who has served, or is currently serving, will understand. This inspirational collection is a must have for all servicemen and women as a reminder that they are not alone, and for the families and loved ones that support them." **William Cannon Hunter, Ph.D., Cultural Studies**

# ACKNOWLEDGEMENTS

My heartfelt gratitude to the women who contributed their stories to this collection, and to all who have served in the United States Armed Forces with selfless dedication. You are my heroes.

Special thanks to the friends and family who encouraged and believed in me throughout the long and often excruciating process of compilation and publication. I couldn't have done it without you.

All my love to my husband, Lou, and our beautiful daughter, Vanessa, whose unwavering devotion and support are appreciated more than words can express. You are the wind beneath my wings.

# Table of Contents

# INTRODUCTION

*"Who could not conquer with such troops as these?"*
General Thomas "Stonewall" Jackson

## A SOLDIER'S PATH

Thirty years ago I enlisted in the United States Army, as eager and impatient to begin a new leg of life's journey as on the day I took my first breath as a squalling newborn in the 2nd General Army Hospital in Landstuhl, Germany.

At the age of eighteen, I dropped out of college with no idea what to do with the rest of my life. Curious and yearning for adventure, I entered the Armed Forces recruiting station in Provo, Utah, and stood looking at the posters of Uncle Sam that lined the walls. "Uncle Sam wants you," they read and promised. "Join the Army and see the world."

At the tail end of the Vietnam War, I hadn't forgotten the more than fifty thousand soldiers who had already given their lives, or the heated protests and reports of bloody news that rocked our nation. Nor could I deny the energy, the overwhelming desire I had at that moment to serve my country, and do whatever I could to preserve freedom.

I was ready to change the world, anxious to take the road least traveled, to emulate my father who had served in the Air Force and raised his children with a sense of patriotism. I knew this was my destiny.

In April 1975, I signed up under the delayed entry program, and just before I headed off for boot camp in August, I was sworn into the United States Army. As goosebumps skittered over my flesh, I stood before the magnificent colors of the United States of America and raised my right arm to a square. With trembling voice, I recited the oath to serve:

> *"I, Michele Hunter, do solemnly swear that I will support and defend the Constitution of the United States against all enemies, foreign and domestic; that I will bear true faith and allegiance to the same; and that I will obey the orders of the President of the United States and the orders of the officers appointed over me, according to the regulations and the Uniform Code of Military Justice. So help me God."*

An official member of the Women's Army Corps, I shipped off to Fort McClellan, Alabama, for eight weeks of basic training, rubbing shoulders with women who hailed from all walks of life, from the Tennessee hills to the Los Angeles suburbs. As I learned about their lives, and their reasons for enlisting, I realized even then our stories were unique to the military and needed to be shared.

Beyond a desire to escape being boxed into an early marriage or a stereotypical career, or even a stalwart plan to take advantage of the military's generous educational benefits, we longed to stand up and be counted. We wanted to make a difference.

Like the women who served before us, we were trailblazers, unfazed by the oppression and discrimination that awaited us behind every door. We pushed forward, strived to excel, and upon graduation day in the fall of 1975, we were not surprised to realize even we had not escaped the momentum of change and progress.

Soon after the end of our training cycle, the United States Army would begin the process of incorporating the Women's Army Corps. The era of the WACs had been earmarked for history, and soon, men and women would train together, serve together. We would all be soldiers – every one.

Even so, changing the mindsets and habits of the military would not be easy. Allowing women in combat units, to enjoy the same promotions and training as their male peers would take many years and scrimmages – as I soon learned.

After the rigors of basic training, I looked forward to attending supply school at Fort Lee, Virginia, before moving on to Germany for permanent duty. I requested this lineup upon enlistment, as revisiting the place of my birth had been at the top of my "things to do" list. Instead, I received orders to Fort Knox, Kentucky.

When I pointed out the grossness of this error, I received the choice of an honorable discharge, or the opportunity to pay for my own airfare to Germany – not an affordable option on my wages.

Since neither choice was viable, I ended up at Fort Knox, right smack in the middle of bussing riots and racial mayhem, with nothing to do but wait for the Army to decide what to do with me.

In the meantime, the country made its first efforts to desegregate schools by bussing black children into white districts, and the violence and discontent in Louisville exploded.

Though soldiers were advised to stay on base for their own safety, emotions ran rampant. During this time, one of the soldiers in my barracks packed his bags and went AWOL to the hills of West Virginia. Another was killed in a drive-by shooting while having a smoke on the porch. And yet another stole a tank and drove it through the side of the post exchange during a drunken rage.

Happy to receive my new orders and board a plane for Alaska, I hoped to find peace and safety amid its icy borders. But at the time, with only a handful of women stationed at Fort Richardson, I faced an entirely new array of battles, ranging from weather to estrogen vs. testosterone.

Trained on the job as a supply clerk, I went to work at the 120th Aviation Company, surrounded by mechanics, Cobra and Chinook pilots, and with no other females with which to collaborate.

The process of typing everything in triplicate on a manual machine – scraping carbon typos with a razor, and blotting errors with white-out – was a slow and painstaking task. Thus, when my unit increased by three women my hopes soared. There would be four pairs of hands to pound keys.

My commander had other plans, however. One overworked typist was enough. He immediately gave these newcomers special duties. A tousled blond with long fingernails and a military occupation skill of generator mechanic landed the job of lifeguard at the post swimming pool. An experienced Huey helicopter crew chief settled behind the desk of the community craft shop, and the enviable task of working on the golf course in the summer, and the ski slopes in the winter went to an enthusiastic athlete with an unstoppable smile. But my pleas for special duty fell on deaf ears, and I remained in the supply room.

Despite those eye-opening, tumultuous days when I first embarked on my path to becoming a soldier, I went on to serve for nearly a decade in the Army and the National Guard. In addition, I achieved the rank of staff sergeant, and met my husband – a soldier who eventually retired in 2002 after thirty-six years of service.

Today, a woman's presence in the military has become a common, acceptable fact. The United States Armed Forces consists of mothers, daughters, sisters, and wives, prepared to offer the ultimate sacrifice as they serve their country, standing side-by-side with their male counterparts in combat. They are fighter pilots, platoon leaders, and commanding officers leading their troops into battle on foreign shores. They have interrogated prisoners and engaged in military intelligence crucial to conquering our enemies and maintaining our freedom.

I am excited to have the opportunity to share some of their stories with you. I hope those of you contemplating enlistment will find this collection inspirational, and those currently serving or who have "been there and done that" will take the time to revel in your own memories as well.

Thank you, servicewomen, for your patriotism, your bravery, and your sense of humor. This book is for you.

Michele Hunter Mirabile

*"Let's Go!"*
President George W. Bush

# ONE

*"Cowards die many times before their deaths;*
*the valiant never taste death but once."*
General Douglas MacArthur

In 1979, Captain Beverly G. Kelley became the first woman to command a Coast Guard cutter. At the end of a thirty-year career, she looks forward to tackling the full-time job of motherhood.

## SECOND CHANCE

In January 1980, particularly horrendous storms plagued Hawaii, and a lot of vessels wound up in trouble.

As commander of the Coast Guard Cutter *Cape Newagen,* I served in Maui when the storms came through. During this time, we went out on a rescue but ended up staying out for four days. As a result, we saved fourteen boats and an enormous number of lives.

On our last case of that time period, a catamaran named *Second Chance* put out an EPIRB (Emergency Position Indicating Radio Beacon) specifying they were in trouble, and giving the signal of their boat and its location.

In keeping with procedure, the Coast Guard sent out a C-130 aircraft to locate the signal, which was several hundred miles north of Oahu, and then vectored our ship. Our supply of food and water was low, and we had just been through a couple of hellish days of weather with twenty-foot seas. We were pretty wiped out from throwing out life rings, pulling people on board and jumping into freezing water, but when I told my crew our help was needed, they didn't hesitate to say, "Let's go!"

When we got on scene, the pilot of the C-130, who happened to be female, called to tell us they needed to leave. They had been circling the boat and keeping an eye on it, and they were low on fuel.

We established communication with the distressed vessel, and I stayed on the radio as we took pumps over to the catamaran in an effort to de-water it. At this point the seas had calmed to a three-to four-foot swell, and the wind had dropped to about ten knots, a significant improvement from the eighty or so we had experienced earlier.

Although conditions were still uncomfortable, the parents decided to stay on their boat and let us take the children, a twelve-year-old boy and a five-year-old girl. Since it would be a lengthy towing evolution, we could give them some stability and warm food, and rotate the parents to and from the cutter as we made our way back to port.

As we tried to take the ship under tow, the pontoons split and the catamaran started going down at a forty-degree lift. My crew grabbed the parents and got out of there. But we hadn't expected the vessel to sink, so we lost the pumps.

When everyone was onboard the mother came up to the bridge. She joined her daughter and then stood looking at me for a moment. "You saved our lives," she said. "And because of you, this little girl will be a woman one day."

I started crying, and my crew started crying, and even now as I tell this story I have tears in my eyes.

Later she said, "You know, when we were in distress I thought the Coast Guard was an all-woman service, because initially the only people I actually spoke to were women."

When my crew looked the family up a year afterward, they were still living on a catamaran in Oahu, that they had once again named *Second Chance*.

Captain Beverly G. Kelley
U.S. Coast Guard

# TWO

*"Wars may be fought with weapons, but they are won by men."*
General George Patton, Jr.

While in the Army, Leslie Watson served as a medic in Iraq and Korea. She is a student, athlete, and perfectionist who credits her determination and stamina to wartime experiences.

## WHITE FLOWERS OF PEACE

Shortly after Operation Iraqi Freedom, while stationed as a medic in Iraq, I accompanied my lieutenant on an excursion to buy some eggs. Carrying bottled water and MREs, we went to a farmhouse he had seen on the corner of a street near our camp.

The house was near a stream, but very small with no electricity or running water. When we first pulled up we didn't see anyone. But when we got out of our vehicle and walked up to the porch, a man came out and greeted us with hesitation.

I was a little wary as well, because I didn't know what might happen. But he was very kind, and when he invited us to sit on the cement porch, children began trickling outside to look at us. They were all quite young. In fact, there turned out to be about fourteen boys and girls, all under the age of ten or eleven. The older girls had their faces covered. And the head wife, along with three others, stayed in the background.

The family served us tea, and brought out a book filled with English and Iraqi phrases. One of the civilians with us spoke Arabic, so we were able to converse quite a bit.

After that initial visit, we stopped by about once a week. We'd bring MREs and Tylenol or other basic medical support, and if they had a medical problem, we'd try to do whatever we could to help.

I always brought candy for the children, and they would run up to me, excited and laughing, even though their father would try to make them leave me alone and behave.

I also brought my journal and colored pencils, and I would set them down on the porch table and try to get the children to draw pictures. At first they wouldn't, so I starting drawing in my journal to let them know it was all right.

Finally, one of the boys drew a dump truck, and after that, the boys drew trucks and the little girls drew flowers of all kinds. Then they wrote their names. Therefore I have their names and their pictures in my journal, in all different colors. And when we left there for the last time, I left those colored pencils with them.

We also left with them some large bolts of fabric from Saddam's palace, as well as shoes and other things they needed. It felt good to be able to show them a little bit of kindness.

Sometimes during our visits to this family, their neighbors would come over to join us for tea. Even though we weren't able to communicate very well, we would all just sit there, smiling and enjoying each other's company, and understanding each other through body language.

On our last visit, when we told them that we wouldn't be coming back, they prepared us a meal of lettuce, tomatoes, potatoes and hard-boiled eggs. And one neighbor, who spoke very good English, gave me a hug and started to cry.

"Americans," he said, "are white flowers of peace."

That meant a lot to us all.

Leslie Watson
U.S. Army

# THREE

The twenty-seventh woman to graduate from flight school, Chief Warrant Officer Cynthia F. Hudgens flew Huey helicopters in the Army. Today she is a full-time Blackhawk pilot for the Army National Guard, and a veteran of Operation Iraqi Freedom. She enjoys running, weight lifting and painting, and collects odd things such as old keys and polished rocks.

## RISKING IT ALL

As a tomboy living in the Deep South (Baton Rouge, Louisiana), I grew up playing Army with all the boys on the block.

Always a nerd in school, I didn't quite fit in. But at the age of thirteen, I discovered the Civil Air Patrol – an auxiliary to the Air Force, often called the flying boy scouts. I loved all the marching and the aviation studies, although the textbooks and technical training were a little over my head at the time. One of the senior members had all the insignias stored in a tackle box, and when I saw the pilot wings in there I thought I could be a pilot and really be somebody.

When I graduated from high school, I wanted to fly for the Air Force. But at the time, women weren't allowed to do that. In addition, I have a borderline astigmatism in my right eye, and since women were just coming in – and back then you had to have perfect vision – every flight surgeon immediately disqualified me.

Although the Air Force kept telling me no, the Army had just started to let women fly. Still, I couldn't pass the damn flight physical due to this teeny bit of astigmatism. But there was always hope in me that wouldn't die, and I couldn't take no for an answer

In 1975, at the age of nineteen and with two years of Air Force ROTC under my belt, I joined the Women's Army Corps to do OH-58 helicopter maintenance. If I couldn't fly, at least I could to do *something* with helicopters.

In the meantime, I reapplied several times for flight school. Although I kept getting turned down and discouraged, deep inside I knew I was meant to fly. So I remained tenacious. And when someone cued me in to a more lenient flight surgeon, my hopes soared.

The day of my exam, the assistant dilated my eyes, and the doctor ran me through the different lenses and said, "Yeah, you're right about that astigmatism, but I don't see that it's a problem."

I couldn't believe my ears! I wanted to kiss that doctor. Finally, after two years of trying and waiting, a flight surgeon had signed me off. I knew it was meant to be.

In May of 1976, I started flight school. It was the 200th year of our nation. The Women's Army Corps was being dissolved, and the Army had announced that women could attend military academy.

Flight school is divided into four phases. Snowbird is pre-flight, the ground school classes before starting actual flight school, followed by primary flight, where we fly a TH-55, a two-seater Plexiglas bubble with three rotor blades on top that are about the width of a ruler. Then we have Huey transition and instruments, and then tactics.

One day, while at primary training, we had a substitute instructor who was kind of rough. The Army's intent behind any school is to get people to quit through emotional harassment. Because if you can't take that kind of stress and abuse, then chances are you won't be able to take the stress of real life and death situations and they don't want you. At the same time, it is difficult to learn in that kind of environment.

We were doing touch-and-go auto rotations, and he made me kind of nervous. So I wasn't doing my best when he said, "We're going to do an auto turn, and I bet you can't land on panel four."

I said, "Okay, show me."

So he takes off, goes downwind, and then turns right back around, skidding the aircraft a length and a half as he lands on the pad.

I thought he was pretty darn good.

Then I took off, and instead of being cool and collected, I was too close to my landing area, so my turn was off and I fell like a duck out of the air. But by the time I had managed to decelerate and touchdown, I'd landed right square on the pad.

That was my first moment of glory as a pilot.

When I finished flight school in May 1977, I became the twenty-seventh woman to graduate. Today, of all pilots and military services, women still only make up about one or two percent.

My first duty assignment was Panama. We flew missions into Honduras and El Salvador, because there was a border dispute going on between the two. But Nicaragua had closed their borders due to the war and we weren't able to fly there, which was inconvenient for us because we had to carry extra fuel tanks.

El Salvador wasn't friendly at all – everybody wore a frown. They had less land and more people, and they kept spilling over into Honduras. Things were the opposite in Honduras, however. Everyone waved at us, and kids ran up to the aircraft after we had shut down.

The most unusual thing I have ever seen from the air was while coming back from Honduras to Panama. We had already refueled in Costa Rica, so we were on the last leg of our journey. The sun sat low over the Western horizon, and it had rained. We were along the coastline and I could see a rainbow. I was in the right seat, and when I looked over at the other pilot I could see a rainbow out his door. I could also see the rainbow down through his chin bubble, up through his greenhouse, out of my greenhouse, and out my door. In fact, it made a complete circle around us.

I joined the Army National Guard in 1985. The Guard treated me better than the Army had at the first of my career, and in some ways was more professional. When I started out there was tremendous resentment toward women, and at the time I resented their resentment. I often wondered what did I do to piss them off?

In 2003, I was deployed to Iraq as a line pilot for six months, in a support battalion, never in front line combat. I did "ash and trash," or junk missions, and used to joke that I was basically a flying deuce-and-a-half truck, because during the first three weeks of the invasion (OIF), we were hopping from one field site to the next.

Essentially we flew water, MREs, and aircraft parts up and down from Kuwait to the different sites, until the Chinook pilots took over because they could carry bigger loads. But once we settled in we did personnel rotations, so people could go on leave. So every other day we would fly from Mosul to Balad, or Baghdad, and the C-130s and C-141s would pick up the troops and take them the rest of the way.

Sometimes we would do missions with Special Forces along the borders, and as far as I know we weren't shot at. And I didn't hear about any Blackhawks getting shot down until I got home. That happened in Mosul, where I had just been.

Two years later, I finally had the opportunity to go to Nicaragua. I spent three weeks there flying support missions for New Horizons 2005. Every morning we would crank up and take the medics for a hop around the area to show them where all the sites were so if we had a call they would know where we would land, and where to go to pick up a patient.

One of the most memorable events of my career occurred the evening of Tuesday, February 4, 1997.

After flying Hueys for twenty years, I had just completed Blackhawk transition, and was in readiness level progression, going from flight school to mission training so I could be qualified to fly missions. I could fly, but only with an instructor pilot until I had been completely checked out.

In preparation for a night training mission with my instructor, CWO Grayson, we had finished our pre-flight and were gathering our gear to head out to the aircraft when we got a call from Hill Air Force Base. An F-16 fighter jet had crashed into the Great Salt Lake, about ten miles north of Wendover, Nevada. The pilots had ejected and were down in the water.

Grayson made all the necessary phone calls, but he couldn't get any authorization. Life Flight was not equipped for water rescue, and we were unprepared for a nighttime medical rescue. But the pilots, who were about one hundred miles away, had already been in the water for thirty minutes. So he made a command decision for us to go out there because it was a matter of life and death.

It was in the hours of darkness by the time Grayson, myself, and three crew chiefs cranked up, got our night-vision goggles checked out, launched, and set out for what we had been told was a downed pilot, or isolated personnel pickup mission.

Grayson gave me the mission tasks as though I was pilot in command, and let me run the radios. Since it was an actual mission, he wanted to be hands-on with the aircraft.

To the south of us, it was a wonderful night. The skies were crystal clear and open. But north, the weather was total crap. There were snow showers and fog over the Great Salt Lake, and we had to launch into that.

We used a Doppler at the time – an inertial navigation system not quite as accurate as GPS. I had the navigation on the map, handled the radios, and coordinated with the calls out of Airport #2 to Air Traffic Control in Salt Lake, as we headed northwest, crossing three mountain ranges.

On that third range, before it opens up to the Great Salt Flats, the lights of an oncoming train completely whited out everything. So we elected to do 360-degree orbits, staying 200 feet above the terrain.

We hit a dense patch of fog, and had started to think we weren't going to make it. The bad thing about night-vision goggles is that they work so well you can punch into a fog bank without warning. They can see through weather up to a point, and then all of a sudden you are in it. And the one place we *didn't* want to be was in a fog bank close to a mountain. We could see the lights of the cars on I-80, but things were bleached out, and when the train finally passed we were able to pick up the lights again, and the fog lifted.

For the longest time we hugged the interstate, because out over open water there are no visual references, and things are very deceptive. I had my head down, swapping the radios back and forth because we had to speak to Clover Control – the Air Force people that controlled that airspace for their fire operations – and the KC-135 that orbited overhead, dropping flares and talking to the pilots on their hand-held radio.

Finally we saw the strobe, and did a right hand turn around it. Now I was on the left, looking out over Wendover.

Grayson didn't want to land on top of the pilots, and we didn't know the depth of the water or if we had mud beneath us, so we wanted to put the tail wheel down first to see if it would dig in. When it glided easily he put the rest of his gear in the water, which turned out to be only about a foot deep, and then hovered slowly forward. But when he did that, the rotor wash pushed the downed pilots frontward, so we stopped.

Two of our crew chiefs got out on either side of our craft and grabbed the guys. The first one to be pulled in was the pilot, who had a broken leg. We brought him on board with his raft, which surprised him because the Air Force doesn't worry about rescue equipment, just personnel.

Just as we got him into the bird, he pointed and yelled, "Look!"

A parachute had started to billow from the water. It was coming up fast, and the other crew chief, still in the water pulling the raft with the flight surgeon, hadn't noticed it behind him, or if he had, he figured it was completely submerged and wouldn't be a problem.

The second crew chief got back into the water to help, and the third crew chief said, "Do you want me to get out there and help?"

I said, "Hell yeah, get out there!"

So all three of them tackled the chute as it billowed. The underside of the rotor blades smacked it several times before they were able to knock it back down. But if it had caught, with all the risers and stuff, it would have cut them all in half.

Because I was the co-pilot, assisting the person actually making the decisions, I never felt like my life was threatened. But it was the eeriest thing, watching that chute billowing up, because the night-vision goggles are like looking through a couple of TV tubes and your mind wants to think, okay, this is a video, this can't be my life, this can't really be happening. And yet at the same time, there's this horror fascination going on, a total disassociation, and it wasn't until the chute had been beaten down that it really hit me that my crew could have been killed.

When they got the chute punched down and wadded together, they pulled the flight surgeon into the aircraft.

The pilots had been in the water for an hour. They had been in contact with the KC-135 the whole time and they seemed to be in pretty good sprits, but now they shivered uncontrollably as their adrenaline shut down and hypothermia set in.

Life Flight told us they were heading into Wendover, so we decided on a patient transfer because there was no heat in the back of the Blackhawk. At that time, Life Flight didn't have night-vision goggles, and due to the weather and the fog they had been unable to go out to the water. With no depth perception it would have been impossible to see those guys. And the strobe with the unaided eye, under those conditions, was just not bright enough to see.

So it took the Blackhawk to rescue them, and Life Flight to keep them alive.

As it turned out, the pilot had a broken tibia and fibula as he had failed to keep his feet and knees together when landing. And the flight surgeon had severe burns.

Apparently the aircraft had flamed out, and the instructor pilot had no idea why. Something had gone wrong during the ejection process as well. Either the seats had been crosswired, or the backseat hadn't been hooked up at all, because when they ejected, the front seat went first. Because the ejection system uses solid rocket fuel, the flames burned the flight surgeon through his flight suit and thermal underwear on the inside of his thigh and stovepiped up his visor.

Later, the pilot told us it was the scariest thing he'd ever been through, although he hated to admit it because he was an instructor pilot with the Air Force Reserve and was never supposed to admit fear, not even in the face of death.

He said popping out into that cold air, with the noise, the rush of wind and the freefall into black had been terrifying.

I've been on many MEDEVAC missions, but never when someone's life depended totally upon our speed and skills. It felt good to really make a difference.

Our guys got the Soldiers Medal for their efforts, and Grayson and I got the Air Medal for superior pilot skills. It was an honor, as it's rare to get that medal in peacetime.

For me, the military was like a calling. Over the years I've had ups and downs, and maybe I didn't always put my best foot forward or fulfill that calling to the best of my abilities. But I'm glad I'm still in, and continuing to improve.

I intend to stay in as long as my health holds up or until they throw me out. I can't imagine doing anything else.

Chief Warrant Officer Four Cynthia F. Hudgens
Army National Guard

# FOUR

*"This will be a different kind of conflict against a different kind of enemy. This is a conflict without battlefields or beachheads, a conflict with opponents who believe they are invisible. Yet they are mistaken. They will be exposed, and they will discover what others in the past have learned: Those who make war against the United States have chosen their own destruction."*
President George W. Bush

Staff Sergeant Melissa L. Binns joined the Army National Guard in 2001. She is a full-time member of the 115th Engineer Battalion, who enjoys camping and outdoor activities. In 2005, she was deployed with her unit to Iraq.

## A DIFFERENT KIND OF ENEMY

When I walked away from my job at the Salt Lake City Parks Department, everyone thought I had lost my mind.

Twenty-four years old and wanting to go to college, I turned in my application and began attending my first course. But when my parents refused to help me financially I was forced to drop out, and soon found myself working seven days a week at three jobs in order to pay rent and car payments.

For three months I struggled to get by, working for Nordstrom Distribution sorting clothes to send to stores across the valley, stocking shelves for Budweiser as a weekend merchandiser, and keeping score at nights for an indoor soccer center.

One night, during a rare moment of spare time while sitting around playing cards and drinking with some of my friends, the subject of joining the Army National Guard came up. Several of them were already members and told me about the benefits, including the fact that the Guard would pay for my education, and full-time jobs were available once I completed basic training.

Desperate for a change, it sounded like a great idea. In fact, it sounded exciting, exactly what I needed to get my life moving in a more positive direction. So I told them I would sign up.

The next day, as I nursed a hangover and priced row after row of clothes at Nordstrom's, I received a telephone call from a National Guard recruiter. He said my friends had referred me, so I agreed to meet with him later that night.

At our meeting, I was immediately impressed by his professional manner, his uniform, and the eight thousand-dollar enlistment bonus he told me about. Suddenly I had never been so serious about my life and my future. At that moment I knew I would join, and I told him I would as long as he could get me on a plane before I lost my nerve.

I signed up as an administrative specialist with big plans on how to spend my bonus money. Even my parents surprised me with their enthusiastic support.

The recruiter followed through with his promise, and two weeks later on the morning of September 11, 2001, I boarded a plane heading from Salt Lake City to Atlanta. From there, I would be bussed to Fort Jackson, South Carolina, for basic training.

The clerk at the Delta terminal had offered us an earlier flight, and we had taken it even though it had a layover in Denver, because I was anxious to get out of Salt Lake and begin my great adventure. Though grateful to be traveling with another recruit – a muscle-bound PFC named Justin, several years older than me – I felt really nervous, shaking and unable to eat, as I had only been on a plane once before at the age of six.

In no time we landed at Denver, where we sat, and sat, and sat in our seats as the plane remained on the runway.

At first I thought this was routine. Then the pilot's voice came over the speakers telling us there had been a security breach and we could not pull to the terminal for a while. She suggested we use our cell phones to find out more information about what was happening.

I'll never forget the lady sitting behind us, the terror in her voice, or the look on her face when she started screaming over and over, "The World Trade Center has been hit!" She was on her cell phone, and later we learned she was from New York, and had friends who worked in the WTC.

Justin and I looked at each other and said, "What's the World Trade Center?" We had no idea.

When we were finally able to disembark, we headed toward the next terminal in order to continue our journey to Atlanta. We caught sight of a television screen in a pub and stopped dead in our tracks, gaping at the footage of a jetliner crashing into a huge building, and wondering how anyone could have done such a horrible thing.

We stood there staring, until we heard a voice over the intercom telling everyone to evacuate the airport immediately. But we had nowhere to go, so we went in search of the pay phones, paced around until one became available, then called the emergency numbers our recruiters had given us. All around, feelings of confusion, anger, and fear were evident on faces and in conversation. People were outraged, and freaking out. They were lined up behind pay phones, renting cars, and hurrying to get out of the airport.

The number was busy. So I called my mother, and after about a thousand tries I reached her. She was frantic. "Are you sure you're okay? Why did you join the military? Where are you?"

I told her I was fine, and I'd call her after I found a place to stay.

As we walked through the airport, looking lost and wondering which direction to go, we ran into a woman from customer service. She took us to her office, introduced us to a handful of other stranded military personnel, and a few hours later put us on a shuttle to the Holiday Inn. But I only had forty dollars and a change of clothes – not enough for the cost of a room – so it was back to the pay phones, and another try at getting through.

This time we were successful, and in no time we each had a nice room with two beds. But rooms were in great demand and we were short of cash. No one wanted to fly home. People were staying in hotels, renting cars and driving to locations as far away as Atlanta. So we decided to share a room – strictly business – and rent the other room to a man who agreed to pay us fifty dollars a night.

As we sat in our room for the next few hours, watching the second plane hit and the buildings fall, I wanted to fight these enemies who threatened my country and my freedom. I felt proud of my decision to join the Army. I knew it was where I belonged.

I called my mother and my unit commander to tell them I was fine, and in Denver. Then we spent the remainder of that night in the Holiday Inn bar.

Every day for the next eight days we booked a flight to Atlanta, and every day it was cancelled. My mom sent me two hundred dollars, so Justin and I rode the buses around town, went to movies and prepared each other for basic by memorizing the General Orders and doing physical training.

Finally we were off to Atlanta. Needless to say I was very nervous on that flight. When we landed, we ate lunch at the USO (Uniformed Services Organization), and watched television while waiting for the bus.

Then we were on our way to basic, where I trained for the next eight weeks with the threat of war hanging over my head and being imbedded into my mind daily. I took all the instruction very seriously, as did everyone else. Every Sunday we bought papers to devour the news, and from time to time our drill sergeants gave us the update, telling us how our comrades were attacking the Taliban and fighting in Afghanistan.

Typically there are sixty soldiers to a platoon. Mine started out with twenty-eight, but by graduation day only seventeen remained. My mom and some of my friends flew to South Carolina for the graduation, and I'll never forget the pride I felt.

Since then, I have found a great career in the Army National Guard, and in eighteen years I hope to enjoy a military retirement.

Now we are at war, and I am deploying for the first time to Iraq in October 2005. I consider it a privilege to be able to do what I signed up to do, and I look forward to the adventures that lie ahead.

Staff Sergeant Melissa L. Binns
Army National Guard

# FIVE

*"From time to time,
the tree of liberty must be watered with the blood of tyrants and
patriots."*
Thomas Jefferson

In 1996, Specialist Chevonne Day left South Africa to attend school in the United States. She applied for citizenship, joined the Army National Guard, and was deployed to Iraq in 2003. Her diversified interests include reading and outdoor activities.

## THE RIGHT TO BEAR ARMS

I was born in South Africa, where national holidays are not recognized, and a general indifference toward patriotism seems to prevail.

Nine years ago I moved to the United States to attend university, and experienced my first Fourth of July celebration. Touched by the passion of the American people, the prevalent display of the flag, and the respect directed toward men and women in uniform, I knew then I wanted to be an American.

It took me six years to trade my green card for U.S. citizenship. To me it was a small miracle, and the moment filled me with excitement. It had been a long, tedious fight, and by the time I had accomplished my dream and been given full rights as a citizen, I was anxious to do what I could to give back to this country.

Taking my right to bear arms to heart, I joined the National Guard as a member of the 19th Special Forces. Shortly afterward, in 2003, I was augmented to the 1457th Combat Engineers, and deployed to Iraq.

On my first night in Baghdad, I was traveling in a convoy ahead of a recovery vehicle carrying a supply of acetylene and oxygen, when it was struck by a rocket-propelled grenade that did not explode.

The lives of eighteen soldiers were spared by that random stroke of chance, and I received a brutal reminder of the fact that we were at war, and the risk of death was part of the package.

For the most part, I found Baghdad to be a modern city with palm trees, and citizens that seemed grateful for our presence – unlike Fallujah, where people flipped us off and yelled obscenities like, "Die, American!"

Initially I served as a mechanic (63B), doing maintenance and recovering broken down vehicles. But six months into deployment I volunteered for a full combat job, helping to maintain security as a gunner.

My mission was to provide support, and about three times a week I assisted troops in transporting civilians and supplies from Iraq to Kuwait. I manned an M-249 SAW (Squad Automatic Weapon), and either sat or stood in an armor-plated gunbox mounted on the back of a Humvee.

It was a twenty-nine hour trip through the inhospitable and endless desert, or ten to eighteen hours by road. For six months of the year the temperature ranged from 128 – 135 degrees in Iraq, and 110 in Kuwait. It didn't help matters that in addition to wearing Kevlar body armor and a helmet, I carried a twenty-three pound loaded weapon, and three to five rolls of 300-round ammo, which amounted to fifty to sixty-five pounds of supplementary weight.

On one of these missions we encountered an attack by an insurgent, lying in wait for us in the grass. Using a remote appliance, he set off an improvised explosive device and then got up and started running.

From the back of the convoy I heard the explosion and saw the flash of light, the smoke, and the flying debris. Following an instant of stark silence and shock my adrenaline kicked in. We were under fire, and I needed no further reminders that I was a soldier trained by the best Army in the world and my job was to defend the members of my convoy.

Generally our orders were to protect ourselves and keep moving. But this time we counterattacked, and soon my ears rang with the sound of gunfire.

When it was all over and the realization of what had just happened sank in, the adrenaline faded and the shaking began.

In the end, one of our soldiers had sustained shrapnel wounds to his face (for which he received a Purple Heart). And I had gained a more intense appreciation for even the small things in life – like home-cooked meals and toilets that flush.

I spent my first Fourth of July as a United States citizen in Baghdad, where I celebrated with my unit at a motivational barbecue, eating a luscious steak in a secured area in the middle of a war zone.

It has been an amazing experience to wear an American uniform, to belong to a country where passion and patriotism are one's birthright.

And it is a thrill for me to see women taking advantage of their rights as a citizen and stepping up to the role of soldier.

Specialist Chevonne Day
Army National Guard

# SIX

*"No man is entitled to the blessings of freedom*
*unless he be vigilant in its preservation."*
General Douglas MacArthur

India Roderick joined the Coast Guard in 1990. During her nine-year enlistment, she married a coastie and was pregnant for every major move. She experienced many adventures, and served for nearly three years aboard the 270-foot cutter *Northland*. Currently, she is pursuing a degree in behavioral science.

## A THANKSGIVING DAY STORY

While serving aboard the Coast Guard Cutter *Northland* (WMEC 904) from 1990 to 1993, we did a great deal of Haitian recovery operations. One of them remains particularly memorable.

The day before Thanksgiving we were underway and patrolling boxes of latitude and longitude for drug interdiction, and Haitian and/or Cuban refugee interdictions, when we were informed of an admiral's plans to fly out from headquarters on a helicopter and join us for the holiday. Although we thought it was a nice gesture for him to choose to spend the day with us rather than his family, it really just added up to more work.

Early Thanksgiving morning, everyone from the newest deck force and engineering guys to the chiefs and officers, were polishing, scrubbing, straightening, and preparing for an inspection-ready tour for the visiting admiral. The cooks were also doubly busy getting the kitchen areas inspection ready, while at the same time trying to prepare the holiday feast for the crew, and the fancier dishes for the Officers Mess guests.

At about 1300 hours, we sighted a Haitian sailboat – a ragged vessel about thirty-five feet long. By now, our ship was so bright and clean the crew almost had to wear sunglasses inside. But work comes before pleasure, so we lowered our small boat, a nineteen-foot rigid hull inflatable (RHI), and it was my turn to be crewman. Along with basic physical maintenance of the ship, as part of the deck force department my duties included running small boats for all of the missions: search and rescue, law enforcement, fisheries boarding, and so on.

Because we didn't want to pull the sailboat alongside the cutter and risk damage to our ship, and because the transfer of people would have been more dangerous that way, we pulled our RHI alongside the sailboat and ferried them from one vessel to the other at about eight or ten at a time.

While this process continued for the next five hours, I stood and kneeled in the bow area handling the lines and the Haitian people as they came out of the sailboat, while doing my best to communicate with them. Most were weak and sick. Many of the women were pregnant, and the stench of sweat and human refuse was overwhelming. I thanked God for each breeze that came my way.

We had been told they spoke a basic version of French, and we had learned some essential words in order to communicate. I even remembered some French from high school, and it came in handy that day. *"Asseyez-vous, s'il vous plait."* I must have said, "Sit down, please," a few hundred times in those five hours.

After each boatload of passengers had been transferred to the RHI, we had to hand them up to the crew on the cutter. The coxswain drove the boat and tried to keep an eye on everything while keeping it balanced and safe, so the engineer and I could move and speak with the passengers. Helping the refugees up the ladder to the ship, however, proved harder than receiving them into the boat.

Then we would go back for another load of people, who would fall on me while trying to get into the RHI. I felt bad for a frail woman, so very pregnant and without the energy to stand up on her own. She collapsed at my feet, and I held her close to me as we traveled the short distance to the ship. But she was too heavy for me to carry up the ladder, so one of my shipmates from the deck stepped down to transport her to safety.

This entire rescue, though, had put a kink in the plans of the visiting admiral. The helicopter carrying our prospective visitor arrived about halfway through the evolution, scaring the people I was trying to load onto the RHI at the time. But with the Haitian refugees on deck, we could not accommodate it.

It circled a few times so the admiral could watch us in action, then it turned, and the dignitaries went back to wherever they had launched.

By the end of the evolution we had transported about 250 Haitian refugees to the helo deck on our ship, where they would stay until we could get them to Guantanamo Bay, Cuba, to be interviewed and processed.

In the meantime, we tried to make them as comfortable as possible by setting up makeshift showers on the side of the flight deck, and giving them wool blankets and plates of red beans and rice. As was often the case, crewmembers donated personal items such as T-shirts, or stuffed animals they had brought on board for that purpose.

With no lights or marking devices, the sailboat was a hazard to navigation, and we didn't want it to wash ashore and risk anyone else trying to sail it. So we poured gasoline onto the boat, then launched a flare and watched it burn.

After securing our boat equipment, I had to take an extra long and extra hot shower – an absolute no-no in normal conditions on a ship – before I could sit down to a meal. The kitchen staff had saved food for the boat crew who had not had time for dinner, where everyone else had been rotated out of their duties to eat.

The food tasted good and I was hungry. But I couldn't dismiss a particular thought that had been running through my head as I helped the scared and desperate passengers who were just trying to make a better life for themselves and their babies: The biggest difference between them and me is where we were born.

"But for the grace of God, go I." Those words rang in my ears. As I tried to enjoy my holiday feast, I thanked God for everything I had received in my life, and for all the trials I had been spared.

India Roderick
U.S. Coast Guard

# SEVEN

*"What counts is not necessarily the size of the dog in the fight –*
*it's the size of the fight in the dog."*
Dwight D. Eisenhower

In 1975, Michele Hunter Mirabile joined the Women's Army Corps. Shortly after her discharge in 1977 she signed up with the Utah Army National Guard, where she met and married her husband of twenty-five years. She loves to read, write, and travel with her family.

## NIGHT MARCH

When I joined the Army I wanted to fly helicopters, but the fact that I was legally blind without my glasses barred me from doing so. As a result, I picked another military occupation skill – a nice, safe job where I would spend my days behind the counter in a supply room – and headed off to boot camp, hoping to be prepared for whatever might come my way.

Several weeks into training at Fort McClellan, Alabama, our drill sergeant stormed into our bay in the middle of the night, noisily rousing us from sleep as she announced we were going for a night march.

I grabbed for my glasses just as my drill sergeant walked down the aisle near my bed. "We'll be wearing our gas masks," she said to me, shooting a disapproving look at my spectacles, "so you won't need those."

Though corrective lenses for our masks had already been ordered, they hadn't been inserted. I wondered if our drill sergeant was aware of that fact. I tried to speak, to protest being turned out into the Alabama night as blind as a newborn kitten, but my drill sergeant was already on the far side of the bay, informing other recruits of her questionable decision to leave eyeglasses behind.

I swallowed my anxiety and decided our drill sergeant knew best. Then I pulled on my uniform, stuffed my feet into my boots, and strapped my gas mask to my thigh. While being herded outside into formation, I gripped my rifle and squinted into the darkness, trying to make sense of the blurry scene around me.

We moved out in single file, leaving the row of sodium vapor lamps behind as we headed down the narrow road toward the swampy woods behind our barracks. I stumbled along, cursing the moonless night, the drizzle of freezing rain, and my feeble, near-sighted vision.

Soon the rain began to thicken, and my feet sank into the soggy roadside soil. Trying to squelch the voice of imminent doom, I strained my ears and followed the sound of swooshing ponchos and crunching boots. The ground rose in an uneven path of mud and gravel and I lost my footing, landing face down in an icy puddle.

I wrestled with my poncho and struggled to my feet, listening for the shuffle of boots in hopes of rejoining my platoon. But the steady rhythm of rain drowned all sounds of life.

Though I tried to make my way down the road, I had become disoriented, and found my route obstructed by trees and underbrush. I could see nothing through the murky night, and whispers of fear had long since swirled into panic.

Loath to break the order of silence, I stood for a long moment in debate, ignoring the tightening cramp in my arm as I clutched my rifle, and listened to the rain trundle down my helmet and splatter on my poncho.

At the sound of clattering rocks and snapping branches, thoughts of alligators and other swamp creatures clogged my mind, and I called out.

A flare lit the night sky and moments later a beam of bright light struck me in the face. "What are you doing out here?" asked my drill sergeant, with a hint of amusement in her voice.

I could do little more than squeak, and was relieved when she took my arm and led me up the embankment and back to the huddled remains of my platoon. They waited about a half-mile up the road for their comrades missing in action – apparently I wasn't the only one who had drifted into the swamp.

After a lecture and a head count, we trudged on through the wilderness. Only this time I held tight to the poncho of the soldier in front of me, determined that nothing short of a natural disaster would loosen my grip, and vowing that contact lenses would be the first purchase I would make on payday.

Michele Hunter Mirabile
Women's Army Corps

# EIGHT

*"There are no secrets to success.*
*It is the result of preparation, hard work, learning from failure."*
Colin Powell

While serving as a member of the 19th Special Forces, Staff Sergeant Dianne C. Reed made history in the spring of 1996, when she parachuted with her father, sister, and two brothers who were members of the same unit. She enjoys quilting, volleyball, and her job as budget analyst for the Utah National Guard.

## ALL IN THE FAMILY

During my first year as a university student, my father, a member of the 19th Special Forces, suggested I join the Linguists and let the National Guard pay for my schooling and further my interest in French.

I agreed to speak to the recruiter. But at our meeting, my father asked me if I'd like to jump out of airplanes instead, with him and my brother Robert, also a member of the 19th Special Forces.

I decided I might as well go all the way. So the next thing I knew, I had a date with basic training in Fort Jackson, South Carolina, on October 7, 1992.

After completing basic and military occupation skills training, I attended Airborne school at Fort Benning, Georgia. Twenty women began the course, but only ten finished.

Training was tough, and on the first day they tried to weed out the weak by dropping a dummy from a 250-foot tower to show us what could happen if we had a malfunction in our parachute.

We ran everywhere in uniforms and boots, and had to carry full canteens. And most of the time the only rest we got was while waiting in line for chow.

During ground week, we learned how to exit an airplane by jumping from a thirty-four foot tower in a mock parachute. The Black Hat, or Airborne trainer, made us stand and exit as though we were in an aircraft, while the Black Hat on the ground judged our performance and either sent us back up to correct our mistakes, or let us take off the harness and sit on the bench until our next turn. My feet hurt, and while learning to keep the parachute harness properly adjusted, I had bruises on my neck and shoulders, and in other places I didn't know you could bruise.

One day, I had to climb the tower five times in a row. The first time, I was so scared I sounded off with somebody else's roster number, and then I exited wrong because I bent my knees. I finally got the hang of it and started to enjoy it. As a result, I got sent up once again for having a smile on my face.

My first jump out of an airplane was just like we had practiced on the ground. I received all the commands and then followed the guy in front of me out. But once the parachute opened and I checked my canopy, it dawned on me what I had just done. I looked back at the plane and said, "You just jumped out of that plane!"

I was so stunned I forgot to count to 4000 as we are supposed to do (1000, 2000, etc.). Then I realized I was about to hit the ground and I'd better prepare to land. Fortunately I didn't hurt myself, but even as I went back to the trucks to turn in my parachute, I was still amazed I had actually jumped.

On a cold clear day while preparing to take my fifth and final jump to be considered fully Airborne qualified, I sat on a plane between my father and brother. My dad jumped first, and when the Black Hat said, "Go!" I did not hesitate. I just went, and my brother followed me out.

I had been highly motivated to graduate, and it was a great feeling to know I had finally made it through training. In some ways I think my determination inspired the guys to work harder. They weren't about to be beaten by a girl.

Special Forces tradition dictates that in order to be truly Airborne, you have to have blood wings, which is when the wings are pinned on your chest and then hit – before putting the backs on – hard enough to cause the prongs to go into your chest.

On graduation day my father was there to give me that special honor. When he hit my chest I teetered, but I didn't fall. The crowd all gasped at once. It was pretty funny. But the best part was that the wings did not go past my sports bra or undershirt. I admit I felt a little disappointed, but I had seen others receive their blood wings and be sore for days.

Afterward, I settled in with the 19th Special Forces, working in administration, and as the senior food operations sergeant. I was excited when I got the opportunity to participate in an Airborne exercise in Korea, with my father, the company first sergeant.

The first day of the jump was overcast. As we boarded the bus to the drop zone we were afraid the weather wouldn't cooperate, but soon the skies cleared, and I got into the balloon with my father and two other soldiers. When a regular aircraft is unavailable, a balloon is used – not a typical hot air balloon. The gas inflates when it is brought out of the hangar, and it has a basket underneath that will hold up to eight Koreans but only four Americans.

The jumpmaster, who told us he'd made over 1,000 jumps, thought it was something special to put a father and a daughter out of a balloon.

Eventually, I worked for Group Support Company, 19th Special Forces Group Airborne, along with my father, my brothers, Robert and James, and my younger sister, Sarah.

I always enjoyed training with my family. We know our limitations and we try to work hard to make sure everyone knows we are not being favored. And I never addressed my father, or my higher-ranking brother by anything but their military titles unless we were away from the company and not talking about company business.

In the spring of 1996, my family made history by jumping together. We were told we were the first family of this size to accomplish this feat, and the press came out in hoards to take pictures and get interviews. It was quite an experience.

For me, the military has been an incredible ride. It has given me confidence, the chance to learn unique skills, and the opportunity to strengthen the bonds of my family.

I am proud to have worn silver wings and a maroon beret, and someday I would like to pin wings on the chest of one of my own children.

Staff Sergeant Dianne C. Reed
Army National Guard

# NINE

*"Some people spend an entire lifetime wondering if they made a difference. The Marines don't have that problem."*
President Ronald Reagan

Staff Sergeant Stephanie D. Small joined the Marine Corps in 1989. As Reserve Administrative Chief, she takes care of all pay entitlements from bonuses to travel settlements. She enjoys camping, fishing, and watching movies with her family.

## MY HAIR'S LONGER THAN YOURS

I spent twelve hellish weeks in boot camp, training at a little place the Marines call Parris Island, South Carolina, from May through July 1989.

Because temperatures were hot and humid, and showers very short and considered a privilege, my bunkie and I deemed leg shaving a waste of time. Beginning the middle of May, we started a hair-growing contest.

Two to three weeks before graduation – almost two months since either of us had shaved – our dress uniforms were fitted.

I stood on a footlocker so the seamstresses could pin my hem straight, and about halfway through the process, this little tiny female Marine suddenly started yelling at the top of her lungs, "What in the hell is all over your legs, recruit?"

I had been busted by one of the meanest, shortest drill instructors on the island, and for a moment I didn't know whether to laugh or cry. She ordered me and my bunkie down from our perches and continued screaming in our faces and pointing at the hair on our legs, telling us how disgusting and gross it was.

That night, we enjoyed a longer-than-usual shower. But afterward, with smooth-shaven legs, we were marched straight down to the sandpit – a giant sandbox where punishments were served – to pay penitence for our lack of lady-like grooming, doing countless push-ups, sit-ups, bends-n-thrusts, and other unpleasant physical activities, for the longest hour of our lives.

I thought I would die in that pit. And I still think twice about not shaving.

Semper Fi!

Staff Sergeant Stephanie D. Small
U.S. Marine Corps

# TEN

*"I can imagine no more rewarding career. And any man who may be asked in this century what he did to make his life worthwhile, I think can respond with a good deal of pride and satisfaction: 'I served in the United States Navy.'"*
President John F. Kennedy

Destiny McLaughlin joined the Navy in 1987, and served on the USS LY *Spear* during the Gulf War. Despite the heartbreak she suffered when leaving her twin sons behind, she would gladly serve her country again. As a veteran of a foreign war, she now works for the federal government.

## UNDERWAY

While serving in the Navy, I was stationed in Hawaii when my twin boys were born in October, 1990. Eleven months later I deployed to the Gulf, leaving the twins, and my husband who had recently left the Marine Corps with a medical discharge, behind with my parents.

Upon deployment, I flew to Bahrain to meet my ship, already out to sea. The temperatures in Kuwait, in excess of one hundred degrees with one hundred percent humidity, were a far cry from what a Wyoming girl was used to. To say the least, it was a cultural shock as I got off the plane and crammed into a bus filled with other sailors who also had no clue what they had gotten themselves into.

My ship, the USS LY *Spear*, a submarine tender which consisted of a crew of approximately 1000 men and 500 women, was appropriately dubbed "The Love Boat." We slept in berthing with two showers, and bunks stacked three high. There were a few unplanned pregnancies along the way, but considering the circumstances we had a small incidence of fraternization.

I was a 2nd Class Weapons Technician. But we couldn't work on weapons underway, and the production of nuclear weapons had been stopped at the time – and that was my specialty – so we either stood watch in aft or forward steering, or gun mount watch on the gun deck with twenty, forty, and fifty-caliber guns.

We also did a roving four-hour security watch, checking each deck a number of times on each shift. With weapons department on security alert, we pretty much slept with our clothes on and our boots unlaced and right next to our feet because no matter the time of day or night we had to be ready to respond to any security alert or drill. This happened quite frequently.

While in port we were able to go about on our own, but we had to be aware of how we presented ourselves in public. Women had to wear slacks, and long-sleeved shirts buttoned up to their necks. We went shopping in Bahrain, Jebel-Ali, and Dubai, because the gold was inexpensive and we could buy pirated copies of American music really cheap, but most of the time we opted to stay on base, or on the ship.

We conducted more than 6,000 repairs during our deployment, on forty-eight ships, and spent a lot of time cleaning up after the Iraqis, and helping to rebuild war-ravaged Kuwait City.

We were each assigned to an area according to our expertise, a pretty humbling experience. The animals at the zoo had been slaughtered, and the children's handicapped school had been bombed, as had the American Embassy. Terrible.

Because our ship was too large to pull into the port of Kuwait, we docked outside in the bay, and throughout the days and nights we could hear the explosions of leftover land mines. And the flies were unbearable. They were all over us and around us, and we could do little except organize details to sweep up dead bugs.

But the children stole our hearts with their smiles, and the gratitude we felt from everyone was a memorable experience in itself. As we prepared to leave, the Empress of Kuwait gave each of our ship members a special limited edition gold coin in appreciation for all we had done.

Underway, we watched movies, went to the gym, or hung out on the helo deck. Once, we passed a floating mine which had been missed by either our forward or port-starboard mine watch. The aft watch caught sight of it and our EOD (Explosive Ordinance Disposal) team went out to defuse it and bring it in.

Also, we were part of the *USS Lincoln* battle group. When she lost a plane over the side, the pilot ejected but the plane went down. Because of security reasons it had to be recovered. So with the assistance of another ship, we were able to retrieve the plane on a night rep mission, and put its remains on our helo deck for display all the way back into the Norfolk Virginia Port.

While I was away from my children they took their first steps, had their first birthday, gave up the bottle, and began speaking sentences. Although I received a lot of video and pictures, it just wasn't the same as being with them. The separation wore on me emotionally and I became very depressed and did a lot of drinking – which only made things worse. Twenty-one at the time, I used partying as a crutch, and between drinking and overeating, I went from about 105 pounds to 145 pounds over a period of three months.

Upon our return home just prior to Christmas 1991, our ship received a Battle "E" award, as well as Southwest Asia and Overseas medals. But my boys didn't recognize me. They didn't want to come to me, and when they cried, it broke my heart.

I knew going into the whole thing, however, that leaving children behind to go to war would be a chance I'd have to take. And though I am still somewhat scarred by the experience, I will always be a sailor at heart.

Destiny McLaughlin
U.S. Navy

# ELEVEN

*"Success demands a high level of logistic and organizational*
*competence."*
General George Patton, Jr.

Commander Kay L. Hartzell served with the Coast Guard from 1973 to 1993, where a strong work ethic and sense of humor saw her through the tough times. In 1979, she became the first woman to command a Coast Guard station. Since her retirement, she has traveled extensively with family and friends.

## YOU'RE SENDING ME WHERE?

Three years out of college and employed as a welfare caseworker, I realized I could not do that type of work for the rest of my life. I decided I needed a change, and applied to the Navy women's officer program in the spring of 1973.

While my application was in progress, I received a call from a female ensign asking if I might be interested in the Coast Guard. I told her I didn't know very much about that organization, or whether or not they enlisted women.

She told me the Coast Guard had recently opened its officer program to include women, and that if selected, I would attend a co-ed Officer Candidate School (OCS) and be trained in the same environment as men – unlike the Navy program that remained separate – and learn to "drive" a ship. I was intrigued, and she called me back four times that day.

Within two weeks, I was in San Francisco being grilled by a panel of three male officers, who answered most of my questions regarding what I could expect at OCS with the standard response of, "Well, we've never had women there, so I don't know."

At the time of my interview, the first OCS class with women was in session, but no female ensigns were in the field. As it turned out, the woman who had initially called me was a direct commission ensign in the Coast Guard Reserve, with a civilian job in the office of Navy Officer Recruiting. She had "borrowed" (with authorization) my Navy application.

In August, I left the heat of Fresno, California, to begin Officer Candidate School in the humidity of Yorktown, Virginia. Mine was the second class since policy had changed to allow females, and consisted of six women and about eighty men.

Stressed to the max during that first week – Hell week – I ran everywhere with a rifle over my head, and did pushups *ad infinitum* for the slightest of infractions. In addition, room inspections over the next seventeen weeks became a daily part of life.

Though we had a locked security drawer for our valuables, we were required to leave our lockers open during the day, and were not allowed to have any type of medical items – no aspirins, no Band-Aids, no nothin'. Since I thought it stupid to go to medical for every little thing, I kept a stash of verboten items in my locked security drawer during the weekdays.

When Saturday rolled around for the inspection where everything had to be open, I would simply move the forbidden stuff to my Tampax box – no male officer would look in there! So in essence I ran a pharmacy out of my locker. Years later, one of my platoon mates returned as an OCS instructor and started looking in Tampax boxes. That was a first, and I told him it was totally unfair.

More than halfway through Officer Candidate School, we had an exceptionally long barracks inspection that actually broke for lunch – normally we were finished by 1100-hours. At the time, my roommate was underway on a ship for the weekend, leaving me alone in the room.

That day we had the two toughest inspectors. While one rifled through my stuff, the other went through my roommate's locker, and summoned the other one over. They were both behind me as I stood staring at a crack in the wall, listening to them shuffle paper.

A moment later I heard, "Hartzell, what the heck is this?"

Still staring at the wall I replied, "I don't know, sir."

"Turn around," he ordered.

Upon turning, I was confronted with the centerfold of the initial issue of *Playgirl*. I said, "It's a *Playgirl*, sir."

"Well, where the hell did she get it?"

"Guys in her platoon gave it to her," I said.

"Do they sell this crap in the exchange?"

"No, sir. But they sell *Playboy*."

The two of them paged through the magazine, and then asked, "Tell us something, do you honestly read this stuff?"

"No sir," I said. "We just look at the pictures."

They awarded me the maximum eight demerits and left the room, all the while chuckling under their breaths.

Another requirement during OCS was daily participation in sports.

My roommate was on a medical hold, making me the only woman when my platoon of nineteen played softball against another platoon. Since we all had to play, I, of course, was relegated to right field.

In the first game, the first and second basemen nearly killed themselves in their efforts to get to any ball before it could get anywhere near me. As a result, I never touched a ball in the first few innings.

Fast forward to my first turn at bat, where I was at the bottom of the lineup – naturally. The bases were loaded with two out. The pitcher called in the outfield and the infield and just lobbed the ball toward the plate.

At that point I decided I would show them a thing or two, and I boomed the ball over the head of the right fielder, clearing the bases. Once I crossed home plate, our coach asked me if I had ever played the game before.

"Yes," I said. "Before coming here, I played on three fast pitch teams. In fact, I played first, short, third, catcher and pitcher."

From that point on I played whatever position I wanted.

In December 1978, the Commandant of the Coast Guard decreed all assignments would be open to women. Until then, there had only been a limited number of ships with co-ed crews.

In January 1979, I received a call from my detailer asking if I might be interested in LORAN (LOng Range Aids to Navigation) duty. Pre-GPS, these stations put out electronic signals to assist ships and planes with navigation. I asked him where he got my name, since the assignment certainly was not on my "dream sheet."

"We're reviewing the records of lieutenants we think are eligible for command," he said, "and you're one of them. And in keeping with the commandant's policy of equal assignment of women, we're looking at you."

Of course I was shocked, since LORAN duty was often seen as a death knell for junior officers, and the locations were somewhat nasty. I stammered about for a response, and eventually said, "But, I don't know anything about electronics."

"You don't need to know anything about electronics," he said, "since you'll have a warrant officer in charge of the equipment. You're there to lead the station."

Still unconvinced, I asked him what stations he had in mind.

He said, "Iwo Jima or Marcus Island."

Gulp. Two islands in the middle of nowhere. I told him I would have to think about it and get back to him. In the back of my mind I thought if he was considering me for transfer, a one-year command would be better than someplace else.

I called one of my mentors to ask his opinion. He was incredulous I hadn't already jumped at the chance. So the next morning I called the detailer and said, "Okay, if you're looking for a volunteer, I'll volunteer for Iwo, but not Marcus."

"I didn't tell you about the Italian station, Lampedusa?" he asked. "Maybe you'd like it better since there is a town on the island and we'll send you to language school."

My mind instantly recalled the "I Love Lucy" segment with Lucy crushing grapes. I envisioned rolling hills, olive trees, and pines. I don't think he ever really told me its location, or that it was a rock – just that it was in Italy. So I said, "Okay, I'll volunteer for

Lampedusa and Iwo but not Marcus" – a triangular spit of land in the middle of nowhere.

I pulled out my trusty National Geographic atlas, and discovered that Lampedusa is just off the coast of Africa, between Malta and Tunisia, and south of Sicily. It is the southernmost point of Europe. Well, I thought, it's still better than Iwo.

Two months later I was told to pack my bags. I would be the first woman to command a station of any kind. Pretty heady stuff. As promised, they sent me to language school in downtown San Francisco – three weeks of intense one-on-one classes, with no English. By the end of the third day, I felt like my brain was being pulled out through my ears.

Since I was one of the few total immersion students and everyone knew me, there was no escape. I'd go to the restroom during the hourly break, and someone from an adjoining stall would call out *"Buon giorno"* or some other thing. I'd be at home and find myself talking to myself in Italian. I even started dreaming in Italian.

The only problems I could foresee were the long break between my language training and my arrival on the island, and the fact that while islanders spoke Italian, they had their own Sicilian dialect, which bears virtually no resemblance to Italian.

Lampedusa is a province of Sicily, and in 1979 the men ruled. Women weren't allowed to drive, and generally stayed at home cooking, cleaning and having kids. They could be seen on the weekly Sunday *pasagiatta* down Via Roma.

The Commanding Officer of the LORAN Station was viewed as one of the most important people on the island. So, on a hot June day in 1979 when the new *commandante* arrived and it was a *donna*, the locals were stunned. How could a woman be the *Commandante de Base de Nato*?

We were a NATO installation. I have often joked that I was the "titular" head of the island – in more ways than one. In addition to myself there were twenty-seven men, including the American crew, and four Italian workers.

Lampedusa was a challenge, but the highlight of my career. Here I was, a thirty-one year old lieutenant in charge of everything. When I arrived, we were considered the worst station in the Mediterranean chain, and by the time I left we were the best. We worked hard, partied hard, and treated everyone like family.

My first day there I wanted to get back on the plane – the station was a physical mess. Though relatively new by Coast Guard standards, previous crews had allowed the place to deteriorate. I was not going to allow that on my watch.

On my initial walk around the base, I came upon the reverse osmosis machine – a system that took two gallons of contaminated water to make one gallon of good. It had a sight glass on it with vials for "Product" and "Reject." The product vial was a rusty orange, the reject vial a clear liquid. I asked my chief engineer why, and he shrugged his shoulders and said it had been like that since his arrival a year before. I then asked, "Don't you think it's a bit strange that the product is orange while the reject is clear?"

"Well," he said, "you've got to be a damn chemist to figure it out."

We took some water samples and sent them to the Navy lab in Naples for analysis. Two weeks later the results came back – our water was totally unfit for human consumption because of the high mineral content. By then my engineer had been medevaced off the island because of a motorbike accident, so two other engineers

51

and I took the system apart and discovered it had been installed backward.

For two years all the bad water had been pumped up to the station, while all the good had flowed down the hill for the sheep and goats. That explained why we had no water pressure or hot water, and why all the pipes were encrusted.

On that same initial walk upon my arrival, I went into the head in the engineering space. The smell of urine was overwhelming. I asked if they ever cleaned the place, and they assured me they did but the smell always lingered.

About a month after my arrival we had a lake behind our administration building. Since it hadn't rained and we were on a virtual desert island, we quickly attributed the situation to a leaking pipe. When we dug up the ground, we found the PVC piping had not been glued together, and water spewed from the joints. Apparently the station had been designed by Americans, and built by Italians with French, German, and Italian parts.

By then we were having all kinds of pipe failures. With that information in hand, we discovered the urinal problem – the discharge pipe had been leaking urine and water into the plaster walls for the life of the station. We managed to get the wall dried out, and the smell subsided.

Months later, I was in my office when one of the engineers called to tell me there had been an accident in engineering. I asked if anyone had been hurt and he said no.

I sprinted down the hill to find a cluster of engineers standing with their hands in their pockets – a typical engineer stance – and staring at a white shiny object that looked vaguely familiar.

Once I got my senses, I realized I was looking at the urinal. It seemed they were working on the pipes, had pressurized them to clean them out, and the urinal had exploded off the wall and bounced into an adjacent space. I thought, Kay, this could be your ticket out! I again confirmed no one had been hurt – but I did fantasize about sending in an accident report that said, "Member dismembered by flying urinal!"

Late in my tour, I received a phone call from the local *carabinieri* that two of my enlisted men had been arrested for carrying dangerous weapons. The brigadier wanted me to come down to the station and help him get to the bottom of things. In 1979 - 1980 the Red Brigade was very active in Italy, and the Italian parliament had passed numerous anti-terrorism laws.

Upon my arrival at the *carabinieri* station, I noticed my two "felons" sheepishly sitting in the lobby, surrounded by policemen. The brigadier explained to me they had been carrying baseball bats wrapped with barbed wire, in a resort area that had recently reported car vandalism – things like broken windows. The *carabinieri* had staked out the place, seen these two lummoxes with baseball bats in hand, and figured they had found the criminals. But when they turned their spotlights on them, they had high-tailed it over the hill.

The brigadier wanted me to impress on them the seriousness of their crime, since one could be arrested for possessing a bullet without a gun. So I asked them, "Pray tell, what were you doing with baseball bats?"

They stammered about and mumbled into their chests, "We were on a werewolf hunt."

I couldn't quite understand so I asked them to repeat their answers. They repeated – more audibly this time – that they were on a werewolf hunt, and continued to explain their story. Two frightened British waitresses had told them about seeing a manlike creature baying at the moon, and being the chivalrous young men they were they had decided to find this creature and beat it to a pulp.

I explained to them that they were lucky to be on the island and not in Milan, because if they ran away from the police up there they'd probably be breathing through their stomachs.

After collecting my thoughts I said, "So, you want me to explain to them in Italian that you were on a werewolf hunt? I really don't believe you in English."

I went into the Italian Rolodex in my head and came up with the explanation that they were hunting a wolf man.

The brigadier and his men looked at me and then started howling.

"*Si, si!*" was all I could get out, and we all had a great laugh.

Throughout my tour, the locals told me I would not be allowed to leave, and that on the day of my departure there would be no plane. I always joked back that I *would* be leaving.

When that day came, we all went to the airport. But when I tried to check in I was told there was no plane. It might come later, but they didn't know.

I laughed and said, "Here, take my bags."

The fellow behind the desk was very apologetic, and essentially said, "Sorry *Commandante*, but there is no plane."

I asked when there would be one, and he shrugged his shoulders and gave one of those typical Italian facial expressions, which generally indicate, "I don't know, and I don't care."

I looked around the terminal and noticed all the Italians were wandering off with their luggage. I thought, this is one heck of a practical joke!

But it wasn't. There really wasn't a plane, and we were told to adjourn to the nearby Bar Roma, and listen for an aircraft. Hours later one arrived, so we trudged back to the airport.

At that time, the airport did not have X-ray machines – just two *carabinieri* who would examine the carry on luggage. I had a rather large camera bag I entrusted to a local to watch while I hugged everyone and made my goodbyes.

Finally, it was time for me to go through the security room, where two of my favorite *carabinieri* met me and told me to open my bag.

I said, "I am the *Commandante* and don't have to open my bag."

One of them looked at me, waved his finger and said, "You *were* the *Commandante*, now open the bag."

I stammered, "S-so you think I have guns or other things in here?"

He unzipped my bag, opened it up and slipped his hand inside. "*Commandante!*" he said, as he withdrew a handgun from my bag. As locals and my guys craned their necks to see what was going on, the other officer jumped into action and handcuffed me, saying that now I would have to stay on the island.

When I asked the young *carabinieri* how he would explain his missing weapon to the brigadier, everyone had a good laugh and I was allowed to continue on, though life after Lampedusa was never as exciting.

Commander Kay L. Hartzell, (retired)
U.S. Coast Guard

# TWELVE

*"If everyone is thinking alike, someone isn't thinking."*
General George Patton, Jr.

For thirteen years, Deborah Holinger served as a skilled air battle manager in the Air Force. She was deployed to the Middle East with her husband during Operation Iraqi Freedom, and forced to leave her babies behind. Today she is busy raising her children, and dabbling in Girl Scouts and PTA.

## THE LADY JAY RANCH

As a junior lieutenant in the Air Force, I picked up the callsign "Lady Jay" due to the fact I had attended the University of Kansas, where the women's basketball team was known as the Lady Jays.

Although I had played some decent basketball in high school, I wasn't good enough to compete at an NCAA Division I school. So as a KU student, I played intramural basketball during the off season with some of my Air Force Reserve Officer Training Corps buddies, and with one or two of the Lady Jays, who played with us often enough to keep up their skills and not break NCAA rules.

I thought "Lady Jay" was a cool callsign, and I wanted to keep it – even though most people just called me Deb back then – when I went to the Air Force Weapons School as a young captain. But if you know anything about the military, you know that you don't always get to pick your own name. You usually get tagged with one because of something not so brilliant you have said or done.

In order to keep a callsign at Weapons School you had to have a really good callsign defense – a good story to back it up – and most of the stories the guys tell involve something distasteful or sexual.

So the story I made up for my defense centered on the fact that the "Lady Jay" callsign was an old family name and not related to KU at all.

I said my great-great grandmother was called "Lady Jay" in Kansas City's Wild West, and ran an establishment known as "The Lady Jay Ranch." And I mentioned that she did her part to ensure the West was won by supporting the local men when they drove their cattle through town by offering them good food, drinks, and "other entertainment."

Because some of the men could not pay with cash, she accepted cattle – thus the ranch – and branded them with "LJ" for the Lady Jay Ranch.

Let's just say I embellished a bit too much, and instead of getting to keep "Lady Jay," I was given "Madam."

Oops!

From that day forward I became known as "Madam" in the Air Force and in the tactics circles I operated in. It is a much remembered callsign, and I would venture to say there are those in the Air Force who do not know Major Deb Holinger, but they know "Madam."

As the only female student at Weapons School for Class 96A, I would tell my friends, "Yep, I'm the Madam, and if you need a guy, I can get you one real cheap. I have fifty-nine brothers here at school with me, ready for a good time."

Deborah Holinger
U.S. Air Force

# THIRTEEN

*"In peace nothing so becomes a man as modest stillness and humility; but when the blast of war blows in our ears, then imitate the action of the tiger; stiffen the sinews, disguise fair nature with hard favored rage . . ."*
William Shakespeare

In 1971, Commander Patricia Rushton joined the Navy Nurse Corps, where she served during the Vietnam War and Desert Storm. At Brigham Young University, she is an associate professor at the College of Nursing, who has compiled and published a book about the experiences of nurses at war.

## WHEN DUTY CALLS

While in my third year at nursing college, I joined the Navy and set out for Newport, Rhode Island, to attend Officer Training School. It was the beginning of many firsts for me: I left home, rode in a cab, and saw the ocean and the biggest ships I'd ever seen in my life – except for in the movies. And the movies don't hold a candle to the real thing.

After graduation, I served at the Philadelphia Naval Hospital working with amputees, and in the emergency room. The East Coast's center for orthopedics and amputees, Philadelphia was a rather old facility consisting of a number of large, open wards with probably twenty beds to a ward but no real walls and sometimes no curtains between beds. The nurses' station sat right in the middle and you could see from one end of the ward to the other.

Standard policy required patients who were physically able to get up at six in the morning, make their beds, and get washed up for breakfast. Part of my job consisted of making sure they were up and going.

Because of the trauma our patients had endured in Vietnam, I was careful to stand at the foot of their beds and only shake the traction bars, due to the likelihood that they would instinctively reach out and strike anyone who happened to surprise them. One morning I woke a young marine missing a leg, startling him so much that he jumped out of bed and crashed to the floor.

After my discharge from active duty in the spring of 1974, I remained in the Navy Reserve, ultimately extending my career for almost twenty-five years.

When Saddam Hussein invaded Kuwait in 1989, my mother was diagnosed with cancer. It had already metastasized to her lungs, and though treatment was offered and explored, both she and I knew she would not be cured.

At the time, I drilled with a Navy Reserve Hospital in Salt Lake City, and it seemed probable I would be mobilized with my unit. Though physically ready to go, I felt concerned about my mother. I knew she would die soon and I wanted to be with her in her last weeks and months. She felt concern as well, but I could not in good conscience ask for a deferral. And we both knew if the recall came, I would go.

I watched as the media publicized story after story of reservists asking for deferrals in hopes of escaping their commitment to serve. Some reasons were understandable, such as family illness or newborn babies. But other reasons were simply excuses. "I can't leave my job," they said. Or, "I don't want to leave my family."

It seemed to me the overwhelming concern of national security should have been a higher priority than personal matters. And it amazed me that despite all the benefits these reservists had enjoyed for years, such as education, extra money and new experiences, they were quick to forget their obligations when the time came to do their duty.

I even heard some colleagues say, "You aren't really going to go if you're called, are you?" They seemed amazed that going could be considered an option.

"Well," I said, "I have been in this canoe club for over twenty years. I think it is a little late to tell them I can't serve."

In the end, however, I was very blessed, as I didn't have to make the difficult decision about whether or not to leave my mother. She passed away in January, 1990, and I was mobilized in February and sent to do support duty at Oak Knoll Naval Hospital in Oakland, California. It was difficult to leave my home, family, and familiar things. Also, I still grieved for my mother, who had been one of the most important people in my life. Though grateful I had a mission to complete, I missed her advice and counsel. But I knew she would have expected and wanted me to do my duty.

Through my experience in the Navy, I learned many valuable skills. In addition to nursing, I leaned how to prioritize, organize, and face emergencies. I also learned how to work hard and get the work done.

If needed, I would pack my bags and serve again.

Commander Patricia Rushton, (retired)
U.S. Navy Nurse Corps Reserve


Dr. Patricia Rushton's full story and other accounts of military nurses can be found in her book, *Latter-day Saint Nurses at War.*

# FOURTEEN

*"It is the unconquerable nature of man*
*and not the nature of the weapon he uses that ensures victory."*
General George Patton, Jr.

Thanks to her training in the Air Force, Dolly A. Garnecki has gained an unwavering sense of commitment and the focus to see a goal through to completion. She is a veteran of Operation Iraqi Freedom, a triathlete, and a full-time graduate student in chiropractic school.

## ALL IN A DAY'S WORK

While serving in the Air Force, I was a flyer in air battle management, and flew in the E-3 AWACS – an Airborne Warning and Control System that provides all-weather surveillance, command, control and communications.

Not long after Operation Iraqi Freedom kicked off, we realized that not only did we have air supremacy, but the enemy wasn't even trying to put up a fight. Our crew began to get bored with the constant mundane routine of the missions, and the practical jokes ensued.

In the midst of a critical transition – flying from enemy airspace into friendly – several crewmembers walked by my console, wearing suspicious smirks as they headed toward the back of the jet where the galley and latrine are located.

The only female on my crew, I'd have to say it's generally the guys who initiate most bathroom humor, so I was extremely curious about what they were doing. But I didn't want to take a break just then, because I was the only person on board doing electronic combat, and we were not yet in friendly airspace.

Pretty soon, I noticed the aircraft commander walking toward the back. Moments later he returned with a funny look on his face, and my curiosity really had me losing concentration.

The *minute* we crossed the border into our ally's country I handed off my radio frequencies to another crewmember to monitor, and went to the back of the jet to investigate, looking in the most obvious location first – the latrine.

Someone had left a lovely turd on the seat.

Actually, I'm quite familiar with the consistency of the chocolate granola bars in our meals ready to eat, and I knew right away that someone had played a very creative joke on the crew.

But a number of crewmembers were rather annoyed, because they had thought it was real, and they hadn't wanted to touch it or remove it, even though they had wanted to go to the bathroom.

Our crew had a good laugh about it for several days.

Dolly A. Garnecki
U.S. Air Force

# FIFTEEN

*"A good plan executed today is better than a perfect plan executed at some indefinite point in the future."*
General George Patton, Jr.

Specialist Dana Hunsaker used her administrative and people skills in an unexpected capacity when she accompanied her National Guard unit to Nicaragua to participate in New Horizons 2005.

## TU ERES MI NOVIA

I consider myself privileged to have been involved in Task Force Chinandega.

When my unit, the 1457th Combat Engineer Battalion, went to Nicaragua for annual training to participate in New Horizons 2005, I got to spend an entire month there. As a way to combine U.S. military training and humanitarian assistance, this exercise began in the 1980s. Our goal was to build four schools and two clinics.

We worked side-by-side with Nicaraguan soldiers who had been put on rotation for the length of our stay. My job was to help run the Tactical Operation Center where I worked in an administrative capacity, keeping up with the paperwork, issuing awards, and out-processing soldiers. One of my tasks required assisting with the strength report. It had to be done on a daily basis, in order to keep track of our troops and inform the Nicaraguans of our location.

During our stay, the temperature soared over a hundred degrees and the humidity remained at about a hundred percent. Though we had flushing toilets and running water, the air conditioning was nothing to brag about. But the locals were friendly, and seemed to be grateful for our assistance. In fact, they were awesome.

We were accompanied by a Nicaraguan soldier every time we left base camp to take food to our soldiers who worked late into the night. My favorite site was Tango Five in Villa Nueva. For three cordobas, or a quarter, the little shoeshine boys polished our boots. It didn't take us long to become acquainted, and soon they were calling me Dana la bonita (Dana the beautiful), and saying, *"Tu eres mi novia."* (You are my girlfriend).

I fell in love with these boys, and on my last visit to Villa Nueva I took treats of cookies and packets of peanut butter and jelly to my little "boyfriends," hoping to get them to sit still long enough for me to have my picture taken with them.

But I needn't have worried about their cooperation. At the count of three, when my first sergeant took our photo, my two favorite shoeshine boys kissed me on the cheek, and our picture is the best souvenir I could ever have imagined.

Specialist Dana M. Hunsaker
Army National Guard

# SIXTEEN

*"It is only by doing things that others have not that one can advance."*
General George Patton, Jr.

When Coral E. Thomas graduated from high school, she wanted to join the Navy. Though she walked into the Air Force recruiting office by mistake, she signed up anyway. She trained as an intelligence specialist, and served as a WAF from 1956 to 1958.

## BLAZING THE TRAIL

When I graduated from high school in 1954 I wanted to join the Navy, as I figured I could leave home and at the same time have a place to live, food to eat, and a certain amount of security.

In those days, however, a female had to be twenty-one to sign up on her own, and my father refused his signature. So instead, I left the farming community I had been raised in, and moved to a larger nearby city to work.

Along the way, I met and dated a nice Catholic boy. I belonged to the Church of Christ, and at that point in my life my family was very anti-Catholic – although a lot of our friends and neighbors were of that faith. Only nineteen, I had no intention of marrying this young man, but I told my father I would if he didn't sign for me to go into the military.

That was all it took. He signed the papers, and I headed off to Detroit to process in. Only I made one error along the way: I went into the wrong office and ended up speaking with an Air Force Recruiter. But since my favorite color was blue and the Air Force wore blue as well as the Navy, I went ahead and enlisted in the Air Force, where I served as a WAF (Women in the Air Force) from 1956 - 1958.

I traveled by train to Lackland AFB in San Antonio, Texas, for basic training, then went on to Shepherd AFB, at Wichita Falls, Texas, for technical training. Even though I was a whiz at typing and had been a telephone operator, the government, in all its wisdom, decided I should be an intelligence specialist. It was a tough school for me, because I had never been able to tell the difference between a Chevy and a Ford, and now I had to learn to identify all kinds of airplanes, Russian and American. Anyway, I made it through.

While at Shepherd, I lived in an open dorm. Some people had a hard time with these conditions, but since I had grown up sharing a bedroom with four sisters, it was no big deal to me. A high fence surrounded the area and we were told it was to keep the guys out, but sometimes we wondered if it was to keep us in. If we had a date with someone on the base, our first sergeant would check them out to make sure they weren't married before we were allowed to go out. She was as bad as a mother hen.

None of us had cars, and times were so innocent back then that when we wanted to go into town we went to the bus stop, where anyone leaving for that direction would stop to pick us up if we were waiting. We had no fear of getting into a stranger's car.

However, it was a different story once we got there, because the townsfolk didn't like the military. I don't know the whole background, but I guess it wasn't unusual in those days. We were told not to wear our uniforms so we wouldn't be recognized as airmen. On base, though, when we went to the Airmen's Club, there was a separate room for WAFs and their dates, so we didn't have to sit in the same area as all the young men who might give us a hard time.

When one of my classmates, a black boy, left for his next assignment some of my friends went to the train station to see him off. I wanted to go with them, but I was told it wouldn't be a good idea for me to be seen telling him goodbye. I couldn't figure out why. But they convinced me not to go, and later when it came my turn to leave, I noticed the "white" bathrooms and "black" bathrooms, as well as both drinking fountains at the station, and it began to dawn on me what was going on. Remember now, I am talking 1956.

When I finished school at Wichita Falls I went to Grandview AFB in Missouri, which was later changed to Richards-Gebaur. I worked in the Command Intelligence Office and was put in charge of the classified library with two of the girls I had gone through technical training with. We had to have top secret clearance to work there, and when it was discovered that one of the girl's parents were from Germany, she got pulled from her duties. Again, this was during the Cold War and things were very different.

Because we were a WAF squadron, and women were separated from men at that time, we had a first sergeant and commander from the WAF squadron and another first sergeant and commander from the command we were assigned to. In both squadrons, duties were assigned by rank. Therefore, where the men had one duty, the women could have two, as a female might have to pull Charge of Quarters in the female dorm and KP with the male squadron.

The worst discrimination was if you became pregnant you were immediately discharged. During the time I served, this was being fought against by a young female lieutenant who was pregnant and didn't want to get out. Although this policy has now changed, I'm not sure if it is for the better.

Housing policies were unfair as well. If a male airman married a civilian, he got the benefit of a higher stipend for married housing. But if a male airman married a WAF, his housing stipend remained the same as a single airman's, because the WAF could live in the barracks. Fortunately this unfairness has been changed.

Of course we didn't have direct deposit or even checks then; we stood in the pay line and got a little envelope with our money in it. It was a standing joke that when you married you either moved up or down in the pay line, as you were paid in alphabetical order.

Also, we had to have a pass to get off base if we planned to go more than a hundred miles away. Now, anyone can go as far as a plane will take them, as long as they are back in time for work.

The military experience for women has undergone so many changes over the years that many young women in the service today have no idea how much they owe those who fought for the rights and benefits they now enjoy. They just take them for granted and want more.

Coral E. Thomas
U.S. Air Force (WAF)

# SEVENTEEN

*"If you can't get them to salute when they should salute*
*and wear the clothes you tell them to wear,*
*how are you going to get them to die for their country?"*
General George Patton, Jr.

Commander Kay L. Hartzell served with the Coast Guard from 1973 to 1993, where a strong work ethic and sense of humor saw her through the tough times. In 1979, she became the first woman to command a Coast Guard station. Since her retirement, she has traveled extensively with family and friends.

## GUESS WHO'S COMING TO DINNER

A newly minted ensign, I received the assignment of Assistant Reserve Training Officer for the Twelfth District Headquarters in San Francisco. It was a very safe position for a woman, since the Coast Guard still struggled with assignment issues for us. Only one other female ensign worked there, in Boating Safety.

Within a few months of my arrival I attended a Dining In – a required event for officers, complete with lots of food and drink, and good-humored roasting of all those in attendance.

At this time, aviators wore khaki uniforms with brown shoes and socks, while ship drivers wore black shoes and socks with their khakis. We also had officers affectionately called "purple sockers" – since they oversaw all aviation and ship operations for the western Pacific.

At one point during the festivities, the captain sitting next to me stood to ask permission to address the mess. "Mr. President," he said to the admiral, "all night I've been listening to members talk about officers in black socks, officers in brown socks, and officers in purple socks. But the thing that disturbs me the most is that tonight we have officers here in pantyhose!"

That brought down the house.

Commander Kay L. Hartzell, (retired)
U.S. Coast Guard

# EIGHTEEN

*" . . . this will not be a campaign of half measures,*
*and we will accept no outcome except victory."*
President George W. Bush

Gunnery Sergeant Julia Watson Passey was the first woman to win the Marine Corps National Rifle Championship. Among her multiple titles and shooting records is her 1998 award of Marine Corps female athlete of the year. She belongs to the Marine Corps Reserve Shooting Team, and teaches marksmanship to marines and civilians around the country. In 2006, she deployed to Iraq.

## THE MAKING OF A NATIONAL CHAMPION

Through what began as a childhood interest to spend time with my father on his hunting trips, I was introduced into the world of competitive shooting. Drawn to high-power over small bore and air rifles, I began competing at the age of sixteen.

While shooting at the National Championships, I became impressed by the skill and presence of the Marine Corps Rifle Team.

I wanted to be on that team, so I enlisted in the Marine Corps and set out to achieve my goal.

I graduated from basic training in February 1995 as the high shooter, and headed off to my military occupation school where I received training as a heavy equipment mechanic. At my first duty station, the 7th Engineer Support Battalion, Camp Pendleton, California, I began working in my MOS, and looking for opportunities to shoot.

When I requested the chance to participate in the Intramural and Division Championships my floor sergeant didn't want me to go, due to our current workload.

But I was persistent. "If you let me go," I said, "I will win the rifle championship."

Unaware of my shooting background or the confidence I had in my abilities, he said, "Okay, Lance Corporal Watson, if you win the rifle at the Intramural, I'll let you shoot Division, too."

When I won, I walked into the maintenance bay with trophy in hand. My sergeant looked at me in disbelief, but he didn't go back on his word.

At Division – the first step to the marine's "Big Team" – I shot well the first day of a two-day aggregate. I let the pressure get to me just a little, but not enough to put me out of the medal bracket. I won High-Tyro for the rifle match, which is the highest scoring new shooter to a Division.

As a result, I placed at Divisions and went on to compete in Marine Championships. There were four Divisions: Far East in Okinawa, Pacific in Hawaii, East Coast in North Carolina, and mine at the West Coast in California. This meant I would shoot against the best in the Marine Corps.

At Marine Championships, an M-14 rifle is used instead of the M-16A2. I felt highly confident in this weapon because it is what I had initially learned to shoot high-power with. This competition is similar to the Division. First we had a few practice days, then individual competition, and finally team competitions.

I shot well during the practice days, posting scores that would allow me to be considered for the "Big Team." But I was so nervous during match day one and two that my knees shook when I tried to shoot offhand. As a result, I did not place. I felt awful, and was certain I wouldn't be selected for the team.

As I stood there crushed and feeling like a failure, the head coach of the rifle team came up to me and said, "Despite not placing, we want to bring you up to Quantico for the summer."

I was so happy I couldn't stop smiling. Of course marines don't smile, but I couldn't help being excited about the fact that I had finally reached my five-year goal to shoot for the Marines.

I spent the summer of 1996 training on the ranges at Quantico, Virginia, in soaring temperatures and insufferable humidity, while wearing a sweatshirt and a leather shooting jacket, and dealing with the mental strain of trying to become good enough to represent the best in the Corps. We fired the M-14, 7.62mm and trained mainly for Interservice and National Championships.

For the 10-Man Team Interservice Match, where each branch of the service puts their ten best on the line, Lance Corporal Grove and I were the first pair to shoot the 200-yard, slow-fire, standing position. Left-handed and considerably shorter than me, he had to face me in order for us to alternate our shots. Normally this wouldn't have been a problem, but adding to our discomfort was General Krulak, the Commandant of the Marine Corps who was visiting the range, and standing right behind us watching every shot we made.

Although we struggled, Grove and I came off the line only dropping two points each.

Our very impressed commandant pulled us aside, commended us on our performance and said, "It's too bad I don't have a set of corporal chevrons, or I'd promote you two right now."

Grove grabbed a set off his shooting stool and handed them to him. We were promoted right there during firing. I remember it being an almost unrealistic feeling as we repeated the Oath and had our chevrons pinned on.

That summer at the National Championships held at Camp Perry, Ohio, I also shot well. I went up on stage many times for special awards like High Woman and High Marine. I even won the Dogs of War trophy, as part of a six-man team. It's funny how the slightest taste of winning makes you want to do even better next time. Though pleased with my performance, I still wanted to be a national champion.

At the end of the summer, I went back to 7th ESB until I received orders assigning me to the Marine Corps Rifle Team for permanent duty.

During the competition season of 1997, however, I ran into many challenges that affected my shooting. I missed a few months of training to recover from a broken wrist, and discovered how much the state of one's personal life can affect the outcome of mental performance.

Though dating and surrounded by people, I felt lonely. I couldn't figure out why I felt unhappy, and why it seemed to affect my performance. Weren't my efforts worthy of winning? Wasn't I trying hard to be a good person, a good marine?

After a year of self-discovery, and realistic inventory of myself and my goals, I decided to get rid of all the negative things in my life. I encircled myself with more uplifting people, places, and atmospheres. I said goodbye to the guy I had been dating and made better use of my time. By the summer of 1998 I was a changed person. Not only did I shoot very well, but I was also content with myself.

Now I was ready to tackle the Nationals.

During the National Trophy Individual match, I was down just one point going back to the 600-yard line. But with every pit change someone asked me about my performance. I didn't want to think about that right now, or about anyone else's performance. I just wanted to shoot well and stay mentally rigid.

The wind and rain were so bad the officials brought in new targets and announced a long cease-fire. While I waited, coaches from the service teams told me where I stood in the running. As if I hadn't already placed high enough expectations on myself to do well, now I had the added burden of other scores to dwell on. In addition, I pulled pits before going to shoot the six, which simply added more comments from others, and more time to think about them before firing.

Finally it was time. But in order to finish the match during daylight, the course had been shortened to ten shots at the six. I also had low light, plenty of rain, and had to guess on a wind call and where to hold my sights on a hazy gray box, and blow the water out of my rear sight just before each shot.

I shot a nine, an eight, a nine, and another nine. I felt I had lost and started to give up. But instead of quitting, I thought, well, that's it. The rest are just for fun – just for me, and no one else.

With that, all the pressure lifted. When I finished I felt defeated for a moment, and then I said to myself, "I did my best, and that's good enough for me." At that point it no longer mattered where I had fared in comparison because I knew I had put my best effort into each shot and I hadn't quit.

Before I had removed my rain-soaked gear from the firing line, a teammate tackled me. "You won!" He hugged me and shook my hand.

"There's no way," I said. "I dropped too many."

More people gathered around and shook my hand, and I started to believe I had actually done it. The most incredible feeling came over me. I had been the best that day, and in the worst conditions, too.

During the award ceremony, each time I made the walk from the back of the auditorium to the lighted stage, I received a standing ovation. As I smiled and looked at the faces in the crowd, I remembered that once, I had been a young girl sitting in those very seats. I thought, today I have come full-circle. I've accomplished what I set out to do.

It is a grand privilege to be the first woman to win the National Championships, and an opportunity I am grateful to have experienced.

Some have asked, "How do you shoot so well?"

First I tell them how I apply the fundamentals of marksmanship. Then I tell them how I apply the fundamentals of life – basic concepts such as hard work, perseverance, and a constant communication with my Maker.

Submitting to His will, and giving thanks to Him who gave me the talent in the first place keeps me humble. I believe that obedience to a higher law and gratitude for my talents has placed me in the winners' circle.

Gunnery Sergeant Julia Watson Passey
U.S. Marine Corps

## THE NATIONAL MATCH COURSE

| Shots Fired | Position | Time Limit | Distance |
|---|---|---|---|
| 10 shots slow-fire | Standing | 10 Minutes | 200 yards |
| 10 shots rapid-fire | Standing to Sitting | 60 Seconds | 200 yards |
| 10 shots rapid-fire | Standing to Prone | 70 Seconds | 300 yards |
| 20 shots slow-fire | Prone | 20 Minutes | 600 yards |

*"The deadliest weapon in the world is a Marine and his rifle."*

General Pershey

# NINETEEN

*"It is easier to find men who will volunteer to die,*
*than to find those who are willing to endure pain with patience."*
Julius Caesar

In 1975, Michele Hunter Mirabile joined the Women's Army Corps. Shortly after her discharge in 1977 she signed up with the Utah Army National Guard, where she met and married her husband of twenty-five years. She loves to read, write, and travel with her family.

## MOVE OVER TOM SAWYER

One exceptionally hot morning while I was stationed with the 120th Aviation Company at Fort Richardson, Alaska, my first sergeant stormed the supply room looking for "volunteers" to police the over-sized yard around our company building.

He was on edge due to an upcoming inspection, and more than a little disgruntled at being shorthanded because of a field exercise. It didn't take him long to round up a posse of personnel who looked like they had nothing better to do than pick up cigarette butts and scraps of paper.

Upon recruitment, I dutifully followed the other volunteers outside. A short while later, when all the garbage had been gathered and properly discarded, I headed back to the supply room and the stack of typing waiting for me on my desk.

As I entered the office, I found my first sergeant sipping a can of Coke and shooting the bull with my supply sergeant. He waved me over and said, "The lawn's getting a little shaggy. Why don't you give it the once-over?"

I gaped. Was he talking to me? I was a supply clerk, and I was certain lawn mowing was not one of my military occupation skills.

He lit a cigarette, took a long drag, and hooked his thumb at the door. "The mower's under the front stairs in the janitor's closet. I'm sure the door's unlocked."

I looked about and stammered, intending to pose an argument or at the least finagle the help of another unsuspecting soldier. But I saw no one else, so I turned on my heels and headed upstairs, wondering what I had done to land such honors. I had mowed plenty of lawns before, and I wasn't afraid of a little hard work. But thoughts of getting all sweaty and then having to sit at my desk for the remainder of the day with no shower did not fill me with enthusiasm.

As fate would have it, the closet was unlocked. And there in the corner, seeming to mock me with its rusty blades and paint-chipped frame sat a prehistoric push mower.

I removed my fatigue jacket and hung it on the doorknob (still wearing my T-shirt, of course), then wrestled the mower from its dark abode, pushed it around to the front of the building, and made a swath across the lawn.

By now word of my assignment had spread, and a cluster of curious soldiers had gathered on the sidewalk. When a chivalrous volunteer stepped forward to save me from the dangers of blisters and broken nails, at first I protested. Then I stepped aside and sought cover in the shade of the building. If he wanted to mow the lawn, why should I stand in his way?

My rescuer made a few cuts through the grass, and was shortly relieved by another soldier, anxious to impress me with his thoughtfulness and well-toned biceps.

Soon the road became clogged with traffic as soldiers slowed to stare at me, the growing chaos, and the line of eager volunteers that had backed around the building.

By the time my first sergeant caught wind of the commotion out on the front lawn and stormed outside to tell me to put on my shirt and come inside, the grass had been mowed, and I was mingling with my newfound admirers and sipping a can of Coke.

Michele Hunter Mirabile
Women's Army Corps

# TWENTY

*"Success is how high you bounce when you hit bottom."*
General George Patton, Jr.

Staff Sergeant Stacey Ann Olson is a single mother of two. Through her own personal struggles and her 2005 – 2006 tour of Iraq, she has learned that nothing in life is unattainable. She strives to be a positive and motivating example for other women who might feel limited due to sex, circumstances, or situation in life.

## THE ROAD LESS TRAVELED

At the age of twenty-six, I was a single mother living in my mother's basement, with everything I had ever worked for locked up in a storage unit.

At the height of my depression, I decided to do something drastic – something I had actually always wanted to do but had never really had the guts. While sitting in my mother's living room, I looked her husband in the eyes and said, "Sign me up. I can't live like this anymore, I'm not getting anywhere."

A full-time technician in the National Guard, he was the best thing that ever happened to my mother and our family. I wish they had met when I was young enough to have benefited from having him as a father – but better late than never.

Knowing what a great career her husband had gained from the military, my mother was incredibly supportive of my decision from the beginning, and offered to take on the responsibilities of babysitting while I went away for training.

I was okay with the idea of "boot camp" right up until I was on the plane, heading to Fort Leonard Wood, Missouri. Then I started wondering why a grown woman with a family would willingly go someplace to be screamed at and beaten down. I started thinking of the worst possible scenarios, and wanted to throw up. In fact, I broke into hot flashes and cold sweats all the way there.

Once there, the first drill sergeant hat I saw scared me to death. But I always finish what I start, and I didn't intend to go home early.

The first week was rough, and the drill sergeants played with the trainees like a bunch of bullies. In addition, my "battle buddy" was a nineteen-year-old juvenile delinquent, and I had to do lots of extra physical training every time she got into trouble.

I finally got brave and asked my drill instructor for a different battle buddy. Drill Sergeant Morris was a single mother as well. We seemed to have some things in common, and I think I actually made her proud when I ended training as Soldier of the Cycle, representing the entire company. Honestly, I don't know how I pulled it off.

For me, the hardest thing was the gas chamber. When I saw the first group of men exit from the chamber with their hair standing on end, snot hanging to their knees and some of them vomiting, I truly saw myself running into the woods screaming, "I'm gay! I'm diabetic! I'm allergic to bee stings!" Anything to get out of it.

But I took a deep breath, and then all of us females got together and vowed to let the boys be weak, because none of us would back out or try to run out of there early. And in the end, the only ones who boobed or tried to escape the chamber early were, naturally, males. Some of them were sent in again, and again – until they behaved and completed the process.

The most embarrassing part of the training was graduation when I went to do a left face while being acknowledged as an outstanding soldier. I stepped on the lip of one shoe with the other foot and almost fell on my rear end. The whole audience said, "ooooohhhhh," as I teetered. I went bright red and made a hasty exit. And then it was on to advanced individual training, where my military occupation skill was a diesel mechanic for track and construction equipment.

Through the experience of basic training, I finally realized a long-lost dream, drew strength and determination from myself I did not know existed, and opened multiple doors of opportunity inaccessible to most women, not to mention a single mother from a welfare background. I would never be the same again.

About six months after basic training, I herniated two discs in my back and had a lower lumbar fusion, earning myself a permanent physical training profile. Though I felt like an invalid and a loser, the events I could not do, like sit-ups and running, I made up for by walking the two and a half mile alternate event with time to spare, and maxing my pushups every time – about fifty push-ups for women.

Eventually I landed a full-time job with the National Guard, and over the next few years completed a Bachelor's degree, and worked my way up to the position of Training NCO, where I made arrangements for schools, arranged billeting for drills, scheduled weapons and training ranges, tracked physicals, and performed other tasks. I played a large role in the family support sector as well.

Finally I could afford my own home, and my first *nice* vehicle – something I had only dreamed of doing before. And despite my new debts, I could spoil my children and give them all the things I'd never had. What an incredible feeling.

Then came the day my unit was put on alert, and ordered to mobilize to Operation Iraqi Freedom.

Talk about a panic. I've never been more stressed or scared.

I got that call the morning after Christmas. My mother's husband was in Iraq and due home in two months. I had been her rock during his deployment, and now she would be mine. I made arrangements for my children to be taken care of, and my bills to be paid, and three weeks later my unit mobilized.

Whew!

The mobilization process is so involved and challenging it leaves little time to wallow in self-pity and thoughts of "what if."

Though I managed to avoid the many love triangles that emerged in our mobilization training, it was entertaining to watch the rituals develop – the possessive behavior men developed toward the female of their choice, and how females used this to their advantage.

In my unit, we have probably one female to every twenty males. Eventually it doesn't seem to matter to many of them if they have a spouse or significant other waiting at home. They will find someone to help them get through this experience. Most will find a new someone in each phase and environment of the deployment, and many will fight over each other's territory.

A great deal of pressure rests on the female gender in this environment, because they are greatly outnumbered and constantly buffeted by the advances of prospective suitors. And, the males tend to grow more protective as time goes on and they miss their own wives or girlfriends back home.

Being so far away from home and everything familiar, it seems natural to turn to someone else for comfort and acceptance. And temptation is rampant as everyone becomes increasingly lonely, bored, stressed, or simply in need of a change whether it be scenery or routine.

However, not all soldiers here are making these kinds of choices, and I have noticed the level of respect increases for those who choose not to partake of the veritable "buffet" in the combat zone.

Out here on the battlefield, I have learned I am capable of far more than I ever thought. We are forced to learn to depend on ourselves, and face the consequences of our actions. Knowing the enemy could be among you feels eerie and exhausting. It is an indescribable emotion to realize you could be the reason another person lives or dies, and you must take that responsibility seriously every moment of every day.

All I know is that no matter what happens out here, I will do everything in my power to watch out for myself and my fellow soldiers, to ensure I make it home to hold my children again. I know ultimately that thoughts of seeing and touching our loved ones is what gets us all through each day.

Not one moment of my military experiences would I trade for anything. I believe I have taught my children that it is important to believe in and stand for something in life; that it is critical to pull your own weight and finish what you start; that education is important to developing a career; that your word is your bond. My daughter might have to fight harder for something she wants, but *nothing* is unattainable. Nothing.

I have learned not to be afraid to run through a door just because I don't know what is behind it. Though it is my goal to survive each endeavor with my dignity intact, sometimes that doesn't happen. But every lesson in my life has been a learning experience, and I grow stronger and wiser with each one.

When I joined the military and became a part of this lifestyle and extended "family" I realized this was what I had been looking for my whole life. I love what I stand for, and that I can make a difference for the people I am supporting here.

I am a woman. I am strong, liberated, and free. And I strive to be a positive and motivating example for other women who feel limited because of their sex, circumstances, or station in life.

Staff Sergeant Stacey Ann Olson
Army National Guard

# TWENTY-ONE

*"Never in the field of human conflict,*
*has so much been owed by so many, to so few."*
Winston Churchill

For thirteen years, Deborah Holinger served as a skilled Air Battle Manager in the Air Force. She was deployed to the Middle East with her husband during Operation Iraqi Freedom, and forced to leave her babies behind. Today she is busy raising her children, and dabbling in Girl Scouts and PTA.

## LEAVING THEM BEHIND

I come from a military family. Both my granddads served in WWII. My dad served in Vietnam and the first Desert Storm; my uncle served in the Air Force; and I have an aunt serving in England right now. As a result of their influence, I enlisted in the Air Force.

As an Air Battle Manager (ABM), I flew in the E-3B/C AWACS (Airborne Warning and Control System) and the E-8 JSTARS (Joint Surveillance Target Attack Radar System), which is a Boeing 707 airframe with air-to-ground radar used to track traffic on the ground. This info is passed on to strike planes, ground troops, intelligence folks, etc.

Because I was in the top five percent of my career field, I was selected to attend the AF Weapons School at Nellis AFB, Nevada– it's like Top Gun for the AF only much, much longer, with a more rigid curriculum and flying schedule. After graduating, I taught at the ABM Schoolhouse for a few years, and then went to Robins AFB to eventually take over their Wing Weapons and Tactics shop.

Consequently, when it came time to take care of business in Iraq, my leadership left most of the planning for our weapons system in my hands.

Since spring of 2002, the possibility of going to Iraq had grown stronger every month. We all knew it was on the horizon.

As the war on terror continued, I became involved in "what if" discussions, and began helping to develop theoretical planning scenarios for our weapons system, the E-8 Joint STARS. I was also pregnant with my second child, a boy due in June, and preparing my two-year-old daughter to become a big sister.

After the birth of my son, and the end of my maternity leave in August, the theoretical planning began to increase. Now conferences and exercises of multiple weapons systems were ongoing, and the best tacticians were called upon to develop a proposed plan – just in case. Though I felt honored to assist in the planning, I wasn't yet sure what it would mean for my family.

Back at my own unit, my job changed from assisting in the Wing Exercises shop to leading the Wing Weapons & Tactics office. This new job threw me right into the front seat of planning a potential conflict in Iraq for our E-8 Joint STARS platform. I started taking short trips across the country to aid in planning conferences and staging exercises. But the trips were hard on our family. I still nursed my son, and since my husband also served in the military, we had to find extra help to take care of the kids outside normal home daycare hours.

On the Monday before Thanksgiving, our wing received some interesting news, and my whole world came to a huge crossroad. A combined Air Operations Center (CAOC) staging exercise had been scheduled to discuss the operational level of war. It had been on the calendar for many months, but our wing had not been asked to participate – until then. Suddenly, the leadership in charge of Air Force affairs in the Middle East (CENTAF) wanted Joint STARS representation at the exercise. And guess who would be in charge of such a CAOC team for the mighty E-8 community? Me.

Overnight, my husband Chris and I learned that not only did we need to deploy for a three-week exercise to South Carolina on the Saturday after Thanksgiving, but we needed to mobility process and be prepared for the possibility of going directly to the Kingdom of Saudi Arabia to work in the CAOC there. That was a lot of information to process on a Monday morning, but things were moving so quickly we didn't have time to think about it – until later that night. Thankfully, my husband's parents, Howard and Susan Holinger, were already planning to visit us for the holiday. So we asked them to come prepared to take Catherine and Jake back to Maine, and we spent the rest of the week preparing a power of attorney and updating our wills.

Though we did not know for certain what would happen in the next few months, we knew we needed to say our goodbyes.

It's hard to describe the many feelings I had. I felt excited and anxious about finally getting to employ all the things I had spent twelve years learning. But my heart had been split into millions of tiny pieces that each said something different. "Don't orphan your children," it said, "just hold them forever and don't let them go." "Be brave, and don't let them see you cry."

I thought childbirth was hard. But the physical pain of bringing them into this world was nothing compared to the emotional pain of leaving them behind. I cried all night. And the next morning, I dried my eyes and we left.

As the leader of our little nine-man team, I put on a warrior face and got us to the exercise. We learned a great deal, and in the end, felt prepared for anything. Fortune smiled on us, however, and we were not part of the many troops that went directly to Saudi Arabia.

We spent Christmas together as a family. Santa found the children just fine in Maine, and the Lord blessed us with a wonderful time of worship and fellowship.

But two days after Christmas, I got a phone call from my boss. It was time to say goodbye to the children again. It had been so hard before I thought I would never be able to get through it a second time. But Philippians 4:13 says, "I can do all things through Him who gives me strength." And divine help enabled me to say goodbye again.

As we left, my whole body shook with tears. Jake was only six months old, and Catherine had just turned three. I would not see them again until late May 2003.

I was one of the first members of our wing to arrive at the Combined Air Operation Center in Saudi Arabia to integrate JSTARS into the Southern Watch, and then Iraqi Freedom mission. We did *really* well as a weapons system, and most of us returned home to promotions, medals, and awards. But I missed a lot of growing up by my kids during those six months. My son got teeth, learned to sit up, to crawl, and to eat with his hands. And even though I made it back just in time for his first birthday, I decided I had missed too much.

Though my time in the military had been incredible and I had really enjoyed my career, it was just too hard on the kids to have mom stay in – especially while dad was still serving. So I made the tough decision to separate from the Air Force upon returning from Iraqi Freedom, after thirteen awesome years.

I loved serving – but I love my kids more.

Deborah Holinger
U.S. Air Force

# TWENTY-TWO

*"Only our individual faith in freedom can keep us free."*
Dwight D. Eisenhower

While in the Army, Leslie Watson served as a medic in Iraq and Korea. She is a student, athlete, and perfectionist, who credits her determination and stamina to wartime experiences.

## CHICKEN SOUP

One of the first days after Operation Iraqi Freedom, my lieutenant and I, along with a couple of civilians who had been contracted to work on our company's radar, decided to wander over to Saddam's palace and look around.

It was incredible. There were marble floors, gold utensils, and cabinets filled with fine china and crystal. My company had crossed the border right after the infantry, so everything was still perfect and in its place, including the plastic-wrapped towels.

We even found a chicken farm. But the chickens were loose and running all around, obviously no longer being looked after. So we all thought it was a great idea when someone said, "Hey, we should take some chickens and make soup!"

We gathered some string and rice sacks that were lying on the ground, and my lieutenant chased after the chickens as they squawked and flapped feathers all over the place. Then he tied their feet together and put them in a bag as I held it open, where they rolled around and tried to get out.

When we had a bag full of chickens, we purchased eggs and potatoes from local farmers at the side of the road. Then we went back to our camp that had been redecorated the day before with some tables from the palace, along with Persian carpeting and a little canopy, and cooked our soup in a pot that had come from the kitchen at the Baghdad airport.

It almost felt like home as we sat there with our battalion commander, our neighbors, and the infantry guys that came over, visiting and eating chicken soup until the sun went down.

Leslie Watson
U.S. Army

# TWENTY-THREE

*"When placed in command – take charge."*
Norman Schwarzkopf

Major Delight Simondi began her military career in 1985 with the Marine Corps, as a ground radio repair specialist. Today she is a full-time executive officer in the Army National Guard. In 2005, she deployed with her unit to Iraq.

## A POWERFUL FORCE BY ANY MEASURE

When I saw the movie, *An Officer and a Gentleman,* I knew this was the life for me. I immediately set about convincing my mother to sign a waiver so I could enlist in the Marine Corps delayed entry program.

The Marine Corps taught me a sense of empowerment. It was a hard four years, but I had wanted the challenge. I learned right away that I didn't react well to being yelled at. I responded better when treated like a human being, and told up front *why* something needed to be done. As a result, today I make every effort to treat my troops with respect and say, "You should do that because . . ."

Six weeks after my discharge from the Marine Corps I joined the Army National Guard, and began working as a full-time administrative clerk.

I fell in love with that part of the military, making sure people got paid, and their orders and awards were processed in a timely manner. Though my days were full, it was one of the most rewarding periods of my career, because I am happiest when I am the busiest, and I feel like I am making a difference.

Shortly after graduation from Officer Candidate School, I was assigned to the 115$^{th}$ Engineer Battalion just in time to see my group mobilized to Iraq. Being left behind as the full-time point of contact was a challenge, but I love my job. I especially enjoy the opportunity to rub shoulders with the public, and was recently involved in a highly successful program to procure federal funds for the community.

As Executive Officer, my job is making sure things get done. I am only five feet two inches in height, and occasionally someone questions my authority or doubts my abilities, but for the most part I am treated with respect.

The hardest part of my job, as with any supervisory position, is personnel management. Having employees with initiative is the greatest gift, and I have one of the finest staffs around. They know their jobs, and when they are given their missions they just go with it.

Now, my unit is once again preparing to be mobilized. I can feel the tension, an underlying current of anxiety and stress. It is affecting everyone in different areas of their lives. Some of us are less patient, spending more money and smoking more than usual. But we are professionals, and we have been through this process before.

Sometimes I get tired, even overwhelmed. But I always remind myself that I am a soldier, and I am here to do my job. And if soldiers aren't complaining from time to time – then something's wrong.

The military has given me a wonderful life and I consider myself blessed, even spoiled. I may be small in stature, but in uniform I'm a member of the United States Armed Forces, and that's a pretty powerful force by any measure.

Major Delight Simondi
Army National Guard

# TWENTY-FOUR

*"We must remember that one man is much the same as another,*
*and that he is best who is trained in the severest school."*
Thucydides

In 1979, Captain Beverly G. Kelley became the first woman to command a Coast Guard cutter. At the end of a thirty-year career, she looks forward to tackling the full-time job of motherhood.

## RENDERING HONORS

On my first patrol as commanding officer of a major Coast Guard combat cutter, we were coming out of Guantanamo Bay, Cuba, and about to pass a Naval ship.

In the military, it is tradition for a junior ship to render honors to a senior ship when they pass each other within 500 feet. This means the crew of the junior ship lines the rails while standing at attention and listening for whistle commands, in order to initiate a salute to the senior ship when the ships are bow to bow. The salute is then canceled by a salute from the senior ship.

For some reason my crew had automatically assumed we were junior, so as we were coming up to this ship, they asked, "Captain, do you want us to man the rails?"

I was pretty senior at that time, so I replied, "Am I junior or senior?"

They didn't know, but still seemed convinced that we were to render honors.

I said, "No, that's not the way it's done. Call over there and find out the date of rank of their commanding officer."

They called over and found out, and then asked me if I wanted them to give the other ship my date.

"No," I said, "not unless they ask."

As it turned out, that commander was one month junior to me, so I was really excited and I kind of smiled.

This didn't go unnoticed by my quartermaster, and he yelled out, "Our captain's senior!"

I ordered my crew to man the rail. Because no one from the other ship had asked for my date of rank, it looked like we were about to have a standoff.

The other ship kept getting closer and closer, and finally, we got a call on the radio. "By the way, what is the date of rank of your commanding officer?"

When they learned they were junior, they started running around and lining up. At this point they had no idea I was a woman, as that information had not been shared.

As we started to pass, we were close enough that I could hear them saying, "Oh shit, it's a woman. We have to render honors to a woman!"

Over the years I'd had a lot of issues with the Navy because of their attitude and the fact that they were so resistant to women – especially in the shipboard environment.

So this was a particularly gratifying moment for me because finally, the Navy had to render honors to me.

Captain Beverly G. Kelley
U.S. Coast Guard

# TWENTY-FIVE

*"The nation that makes a great distinction between its scholars
and its warriors will have its thinking done by cowards
and its fighting done by fools."*
Thucydides

Thanks to her training in the Air Force, Dolly A. Garnecki has gained an unwavering sense of commitment and the focus to see a goal through to its completion. She is a veteran of Operation Iraqi Freedom, a triathlete, and a full-time graduate student in chiropractic school.

## GROWING PAINS

My great-uncle flew B-29s in WWII, and his wife was a nurse in the Army Air Corps. They both spoke warmly of their experiences in the service. So when I was pre-med and preparing to apply for medical schools, I listened when he told me about the flight surgeon specialty and suggested I give the Air Force Reserve Officer Training Corps (AFROTC) a try because I could still be a doctor and fly.

In fact, I thought those two jobs sounded like a fun career combination, so I signed up and began ROTC my first year at University of Texas at Austin, in the fall of 1996.

Prior to that, however, at the age of sixteen, I had attended college at the Texas Academy of Mathematics and Science, and lived in a dorm on the campus of the University of North Texas. I carried a heavy load of classes, and by the time I had graduated with a high school diploma, I had acquired more than sixty hours of college credit in math and sciences, as well as other disciplines like history, English, political science, foreign language, etc. When I began ROTC at UT Austin, I was a third class, or sophomore-year cadet, but academically I was classified as a junior at the university.

All this meant was while I studied college courses at the Academy for my last two years of high school, that's *exactly* what I did. I spent *all* my time studying and doing school activities. We weren't allowed to compete in athletics or state-sanctioned competitions against other high schools, so by my junior year I no longer worked out or did sports, and I'd gained twenty-five pounds and three sizes.

This was my physical status when I began AFROTC, and as a result, I failed my physical fitness test the first two times.

I had to work extra hard to pass it my first year in order to remain in the program and be a viable candidate for field training – a necessary requirement for commissioning and enlistment.

But I was determined to make it. And because of the discipline, the high standards of self – honor, ethics, and attention to detail – taught and ingrained into us in ROTC, by my final year I was training year-round to compete in an inter-service endurance race called the Marine Leatherneck Ironman Challenge on the UT campus. I also competed in various road race events.

As a result, I went from scoring a measly 160-170, to a 420-plus score on the physical fitness test in my last semester of ROTC. To pass, I needed approximately 180 points out of a perfect 500.

In May of 1999, I received my commission. The transition from university student /cadet to active duty second lieutenant came with its own set of growing pains. But they were tempered with great jobs and fun first year experiences – including the ride of my life.

I was assigned to the booming Air Battle Manager (ABM) career field – planning, organizing, and directing operations, including airspace management, air defense, and tactical missions – which was a critically manned field as well as one on the brink of becoming "rated" just like pilots and navigators.

Since headquarters assigned new lieutenants to the career field faster than the tech school could train us, over the next two years we experienced bottlenecks. Fortunately, while I waited out the five months at Tyndall AFB to begin training, I was assigned to the 95th fighter squadron.

Initially, I was one of two female officers in a squadron that had over 100 personnel. Yeah, the guys gave me a hard time, but I didn't take it personally, and I gave them a hard time back. Soon enough, I was in their good graces, and they invited me to their bro-bonding time socials.

I became a "good ol' boy" and learned all about their fighter pilot culture, and all I had to do was repair their computers and help with the squadron local area network. In return, they awarded me with a medal and a familiarization flight on an F-15C (air-to-air combat fighter jet), which was one of the most incredible experiences I've ever had.

I also puked into my oxygen mask, a horrible place to puke because I had to smell the vomit for the duration of the flight. I pulled 7.8 Gs on that unforgettable ride, and even though I've never been drunk, afterward I felt like what must have been similar to a very nasty and painful hangover.

In 2003, as a member of the 552nd AWACS Operations Group, I was deployed to Prince Sultan Air Base, Saudi Arabia, in support of Operations Southern Watch. During my seventy-seven days there, the rules of engagement changed to wartime and became Operation Iraqi Freedom. As a result, I was there when the war began.

An electronic combat officer, it was exciting to finally be able to do what I'd been training to do for years. At the same time, it was frightening not knowing what to expect in a wartime situation. I wondered what threats we would face in the air or on the ground, or if I would see family and loved ones again. Would my husband – who had also been deployed – or I be widowed at war? Would I see death, or indirectly cause it?

A devout Christian, I suggested to my commander the idea of praying as a crew. He liked the idea, and soon it became a routine task before each flight to gather in a circle as a crew and bow our heads in prayer. During the harshness of war, it prepared our mental and spiritual focus, and reminded us of God's glory and purpose when our situation was grim or uncomfortable, or when we were frustrated with decisions or each other.

Despite the difficulties of deployment, my time in the desert during OIF was a time of spiritual growth. Away from the daily routine of life, I had time to focus more on God, my blessings and cherished friendships, and to reflect upon His word and the many wondrous works He's doing in my life and in the lives of those around me.

The Air Force taught me countless lessons and qualities, including an unwavering sense of commitment and the focus to see a goal through to its completion. Today, following five years on active duty, I am a full-time grad student in chiropractic school. These traits are invaluable to me now.

Dolly A. Garnecki
U.S. Air Force

# TWENTY-SIX

*" . . . If you leave here with the word DUTY implanted in your mind; if you leave here with the word HONOR carved in your soul; if you leave here with love of COUNTRY stamped on your heart, then you will be a twenty-first century leader worthy . . . of the great privilege and honor . . . of leading . . . the sons and daughters of America . . ."*
General H. Norman Schwarzkopf

Captain April Bennett joined the Army on a dare, and trained as a medic before attending Officer Candidate School. She is a veteran of Operation Enduring Freedom, and holds the full-time position of Deputy State Surgeon in the Utah Army National Guard.

## THE ULTIMATE COMPLIMENT

In February 2003, the 1457th Combat Engineer Battalion was mobilized and sent to Iraq. Our mission was to go into Baghdad, establish a secure area, and build it.

There were twelve women in our battalion of 425 including me, the only female officer, a second lieutenant assigned as Support Leader/Executive Officer of Support Company.

Early on the morning of May 28th, we arrived in Baghdad. We had driven all through the night, and we were tired and scared. None of us had ever been deployed before, and we wondered what in the world we had gotten ourselves into.

Just as we rolled into the city, a rocket struck one of the rear vehicles of our convoy. Fortunately it was a dud and didn't go off, but we stopped and returned small arms fire.

We couldn't see anything because it was still dark, so we waited for a while in dead silence, gathering our thoughts, and lying on the ground with our weapons pointed out. Then we proceeded down the road toward the airport, and by the time we got there, those who had been shaken up by the incident had had time to talk about it and get it squared away.

By now the sun had started to rise, and we looked around not knowing what to expect. First we saw the big swords, or crossed sabers of Saddam, and then all the destruction. It looked like a big hurricane had blown through there. Trees were uprooted and burned, buildings blown up. And all around us lay unexploded ordinance and debris. It was unbelievable.

We were one of the first engineer units to arrive in the area, so we were directed to a huge wheat field and told, "Okay, here you go. This is where you're going to live. Fix it up."

Our first night no one could sleep. It would be so quiet, and then all of a sudden we would hear strange noises and barking dogs.

We tried to nap the next day but the heat made it impossible. The temperature soared to 145. And even by midnight, with the sun down, it was 100 degrees. Plus, we had to wear all of our gear. Although we didn't have to sleep with it, it had to remain nearby at all times. We even slept in our fatigues – until we got a little more comfortable with things, if you can ever get comfortable in an environment like that.

While we set up, other units arrived. Across the dirt road was a Patriot Missile Battery, and about a half-mile to the west were the landing strip and the Air Force.

It took us a couple of days to clear the area of explosives. Then we graded it with our heavy equipment, spread out a layer of rocks, and set up tents. Each tent held six to ten men. We had two tents for females. I had my own, which left the other tent crowded. So I shared with two females for a while.

At first everyone slept on cots. But as time went on, we had access to wood and started building our own beds. We got on the Internet when we could and ordered Coleman mattresses, or went to the little stores run by locals we called hodgies, and bought two or three flat mattresses to stack up.

We built bathrooms with wooden walls, porta-johns, and barrels we cut in half. And we used our canteens and bottled water for sponge baths, because there were no showers.

For the first three months we ate MREs for every meal. We learned some creative ways to eat them, and we'd trade peanut butter and cheese, and make things with crackers. Then our cooks prepared us two meals a day for about a month. But they were awful, simply because of the limited ingredients available. Finally, the Army contracted cooks to come in, and we had three decent meals a day in the mess hall.

We pulled security around our own perimeter, as well as other areas. Our camp was the most eastern edge, and right outside our wall sat a tank. The sound of mortars, gunfire, and explosions of all kinds were endless and unnerving. But we got used to it.

As platoon leader for Support Company I did convoys, and kept track of the medics, cooks, and communication section. My platoon also provided anything needed supply wise, such as barriers, etc.

Day and night we carried our weapons, and had to clean them often because of the sand and wind. At the beginning of my deployment I carried an M-16, which I preferred for its firepower. And for the last part, I wore a 9mm in a shoulder holster.

The training and ages of our battalion were very diverse. Women were aged from nineteen to forty-eight years old, and had military occupation skills ranging from mechanic to medic to administration. We bonded really well and took care of each other. Even to this day we are good friends.

For the most part our battalion adapted and became cohesive, because we had no idea how long we would be there. But over the months, as we started getting anxious to go home and our demeanor diminished, we got on each other's nerves.

I had a lot of support from family and friends, and received many letters, e-mails, and packages. Like everyone else, at first I wanted Gatorade, toilet paper, and baby wipes. Later I craved hot sauce, hot chocolate, macaroni and cheese, and tuna fish.

Eventually the locals set up shops in the green zone, where we could buy all kinds of things such as food, jewelry, blankets, pillows, paintings, and electronics – including televisions.

Since we were engineers, we built power, and got big generators that put electricity and air conditioning in our tents. We became pretty sophisticated, except for the fact that we had to wash our clothes by hand. We thought we were getting them nice and clean, but now as I look back at pictures of our water, they were probably filthy.

For the most part we felt safe around the locals. Some of them were grateful we were there, and others thought we had no business there at all. Sometimes we got looks that made us feel uncomfortable. And occasionally someone would yell at us, but we couldn't understand them.

We built a range on the other side of the city, so we had to convoy through Baghdad, staying on the outskirts of the metropolis to get to the other side. One morning our convoy commander took a wrong turn, and we drove into town on what we would consider a roundabout. But we couldn't find our way out, so we had to circle again.

People came into the streets, and men screamed and yelled at us. We started getting pretty nervous, but we finally found our turn and got out of there.

After that we learned different routes, and traveled through the city at various times of day. I ran a lot of convoys myself, and sometimes I would leave before daylight. A convoy always consisted of at least three vehicles, but I usually had seven, ten, or even fifteen. As convoy commander I briefed the route, and accounted for personnel, trucks, and equipment. I also had an NCO to assist me. He would travel at the rear, and I would be at the front. In addition, I had a driver, and a gun truck for security that used a 50 Cal, or a SAW.

These convoys were very, very scary, and in the beginning I had no idea where to go. The first thing I did every morning before we left was to find out if any IED's or action had happened on any of our routes.

It was a big responsibility, but I had really good soldiers that listened to me, and were willing and cooperative. We worked as a team, because that is the only way to survive out there.

Although we drove in the dark, it was about a hundred degrees. We had to cross a bridge over the Tigris River, and we were always excited to get to that point because a big rush of cool air would wash over us, and it felt so good. And then we would get off the bridge and it was so hot again.

The Tigris is polluted and filthy. Everything including the sewer dumps into it. There are a lot of sandbars as well, and in some places you can actually walk out into the river.

For about eight weeks, I did a convoy every other day. We learned all the back streets, and knew how long each route would take us. In all my convoys I never lost a vehicle, or had any kind of injuries.

One day, while traveling with my commander and about eighteen vehicles, one of them broke down. The convoy split up, and we had about a half-mile between us.

As assistant convoy commander, I was at the back. We had stopped, and were trying to fix a flat tire when we heard gunfire. Ricochet hit right by us. I'd never been shot at before, and I just freaked out and got on the radio. "Sir," I said to my commander, "we're taking fire."

He said, "Okay, we'll back up. Make sure everyone's under cover, but keep working on the tire."

There were a lot of buildings around us but we couldn't see anybody. And thank God I never had to fire my weapon at anyone. Despite the fact that we were really nervous and in a panic, we all remembered what to do.

We'd trained in this scenario so many times that everyone automatically followed procedure. We put a sheet of steel by the tire to protect the soldier working on it, made sure everyone was okay, changed the tire, got moving on the road, and called in the incident. It was remarkable how quickly our natural instincts kicked in.

Another time we went into town to get some parts. The sun was glaring, and people stared at us. They don't say anything; they just stare at you. While we pulled security outside of the store, in a very busy road, two cars crashed right in front of us, trapping our convoy in that area.

When the drivers got out of their vehicles and started yelling at each other, I immediately suspected they were trying to create a diversion.

Finally one of our NCOs walked over and told them to get their vehicles out of the way. But they didn't pay attention, so the rest of us went over there, pointed our weapons down at the ground and said, "You need to get out of here. Move these vehicles now."

All of a sudden we heard gunfire behind us and in the alleys. Around us people were yelling, "Ali Baba! Ali Baba!" Which over there meant bad guy. We were so scared. By the time they had moved their vehicles, those shots were pretty close.

Many of the situations I experienced were close calls, and I had some trouble sleeping for a few days afterward. But I would try to talk myself out of it and think happy thoughts.

When I went home on a two-week leave, I couldn't sleep because it was so quiet. I heard every little noise, and kept wondering where I'd put my weapon. One day, while talking on the phone with one of my platoon sergeants in Iraq, I heard all this gunfire in the background. When I asked him about the commotion, he said, "We just found Saddam."

"No way!" I said, turning on CNN. But sure enough, we'd caught Saddam.

It was pretty bizarre, sitting there listening to gunfire on the phone while hearing it on the news. And I kept thinking, "Oh my gosh, that's where I live!"

In addition to our military training as combat engineers, as National Guardsmen we brought civilian skills to the table that were very helpful to our missions, ranging from police officer to nurse to contractor to all kinds of actual engineers. As a result, we got a lot of experience searching tunnels, surveying, rebuilding bridges, and building schools.

Attached to our battalion was a boat detachment from Fort Lewis. I had the opportunity to accompany them on a river patrol. Our mission was to gather the grid coordinates of all the damaged boats and yachts blocking the river so they could be removed.

As we traveled along, the other boat with us hit a sandbar and stopped suddenly. We had to stop and pull it out, a scary ordeal because of all the people living along the shore in everything from little mud huts to gorgeous palaces. Fortunately, the detachment we were with had patrolled the river during the war so they were familiar with the area.

We also stopped at a house to drop off MREs, because the resident had helped earlier to detect a machine-gun nest, and his cooperation had saved a bunch of lives. So we took good care of this family and he was happy to see us. Although we were supposed to follow certain rules, we couldn't help being human. We dug in our pockets for candy and change for the children, and their beautiful smiles were our reward.

After a while, the AAFES centers set up a PX, as well as a Burger King. We were pretty excited, and the burgers were the best ever. We also had a basketball and volleyball court, as well as a small weight room.

While we were in Iraq, newscasters from CNN ran a story on the Engineers. One of them asked me, "What's the first thing you're going to do when you get home?"

I said, "I'm going to flush a toilet."

He thought that was the funniest thing he had ever heard.

"You have no idea what it's like to go into those porta-johns in 130 degree temperatures," I said. "It is horrible. I cannot wait!"

They would come and dump them all at about the same time, and we'd say, "Oh, it's shitter cocktail time." The stench was stale, and constant. Sometimes even now I can smell it.

The Assassin's Gate is a huge arch going into the green zone. On our side, we called it the gate to freedom. On the other side, we called it the gate to hell. One of our first nights in Iraq, I climbed to the top of the gateway with several of my friends. As we lay on the roof overlooking Baghdad in the heat and the dark, we could hear gunfire. We said how we couldn't wait to get home and sit at the bar, tip our beers and say, "Here's to sitting on that gate in Baghdad."

When we got home in April 2004, we had a beer at the bar, and as we toasted we closed our eyes and remembered that night up on top of the Assassin's Gate. It was the best beer I have ever had.

We've been home now for about a year and a half, and there are a lot of us who still have bad dreams. But life is weird. And it has a way of going on without you.

Though several of our soldiers were wounded by shrapnel or exploding IED's, and one was even diagnosed with leukemia, we brought everybody home.

Some of us didn't believe in why we were there, and some of us absolutely believed in why we were there. But it didn't matter.

We were there for a cause, and nobody questioned. We just did our jobs. We did what we were supposed to do and looked out for each other, and as a result, 425 of us came back home.

We were called the Mormon Battalion. I believe we had a lot of spiritual protection, and that the Lord was always with us.

You can only get out of something what you put into it. If you take your heart and soul over there, you're going to get your heart and soul back. And I wouldn't trade the bonds, the feelings, or the honor I experienced because I fought for my country.

As a woman, I was never judged or had any problems whatsoever with soldiers of any age. I received positive feedback from men and women alike, saying they felt safe and secure with me because they believed in me. "She's a soldier," they said, "and she will cover my back and do whatever she can to make sure I am safe."

As an officer, the ultimate compliment was hearing my people say, "You know what? I'll take that lieutenant with me anywhere."

Captain April Bennett
Army National Guard


*"The eyes of the world are upon you.*
*The hopes and prayers of liberty-loving people everywhere march*
*with you."*
General Dwight D. Eisenhower

# TWENTY-SEVEN

*"I am not bound to win, but I am bound to be true. I am not bound to succeed, but I am bound to live by the light that I have. I must stand with anybody that stands right, stand with him while he is right, and part with him when he goes wrong."*
Abraham Lincoln

Commander Kay L. Hartzell served with the Coast Guard from 1973 to 1993, where a strong work ethic and sense of humor saw her through the tough times. In 1979, she became the first woman to command a Coast Guard station. Since her retirement, she has traveled extensively with family and friends.

## JUST CALL ME MA'AM

Early in my tour at the Twelfth District Headquarters in San Francisco, I attended a meeting where a female WWII veteran was present. Throughout the meeting she kept calling me "Sir."

During a break, I told her that I was not a sir.

She responded that Captain X (a female reservist on active duty) insisted on being called "Sir" since that was what Coast Guard regulations called for.

"Well," I said, "I've never been a sir, don't expect to be a sir, and you can just call me ma'am or ensign."

During that same time frame, the office yeoman had been trained to answer the phone with, "Thank you for calling XYZ, how can I help you, sir?" I guess the leadership hadn't realized that women occasionally called the district office, so that policy finally changed.

About a year later, I was president of the local chapter of the Reserve Officers Association. There were only two Coast Guard chapters in California. One day, I received a letter addressed to me with the salutation, "Dear Sir," and the opening line of, "As you two gentlemen are well aware…"

I knew the originator of the letter, called him, and asked him why he would send me a letter addressed with "Dear Sir?" His response was that his secretary did the letters, and really didn't know that there were women officers in the Coast Guard. He apologized, said it wouldn't happen again, and a few days later I received a personalized coffee mug with a Coast Guard stripe and the inscription "Sir Kay."

From that point on Sir Kay became my moniker, and my parents even gave me personalized auto plates for my twenty-seventh birthday.

A few years later, I got another dream assignment as the executive officer for all the Coast Guard units in the Florida Keys, and I was sent to Key West during the height of the drug wars, where typical marijuana seizures were multiple tons.

One day the commandant and his wife were visiting. I knew them from San Francisco. We had lunch at my commanding officer's home, and at one point, Mrs. Commandant said she had noted my license plate – SIR KAY – and wanted to know its significance.

I said, "Despite the fact that women have been on active duty for over ten years, the Coast Guard Personnel Manual has a section entitled 'Manner of Addressing Officers' that clearly states all officers below the rank of commander shall be addressed as 'Sir.'"

She looked at her husband and said, "Jim, is that true?"

While puffing on his pipe, he acknowledged that if I said so, it was probably true. But in defense of the folks responsible for maintaining the manual, he said changing it would be a very expensive proposition.

I chuckled and told him I understood, and that the policy hadn't been an issue with me until the paragraph directly above it had been changed to authorize the new rank of commodore. I added that whoever was responsible for that change had a duty to check the entire page to see if anything else needed to be modified.

Well, the manual was changed within three months.

Commander Kay L. Hartzell, (retired)
U.S. Coast Guard

# TWENTY-EIGHT

*"We must take the battle to the enemy,*
*disrupt his plans and confront the worst threats before they*
*emerge."*
President George W. Bush

In 1975, Michele Hunter Mirabile joined the Women's Army Corps. Shortly after her discharge in 1977 she signed up with the Utah Army National Guard, where she met and married her husband of twenty-five years. She loves to read, write, and travel with her family.

## EVEN ACHILLES HAD HIS HEEL

Dugway Proving Ground is a cold and dismal place when the sun dips below the horizon. While training there one summer with Utah National Guard's 396th Aviation Company, I lay huddled beneath a layer of sleeping bags on a cot in the back of a deuce-and-a-half, listening to the unfamiliar sounds of the night. I hoped the rustling in the corners came from kangaroo rats, not rattlesnakes.

Restless, I decided to make a trip to the latrine – a portable toilet mounted on a flatbed truck, parked in the center of a circle of forty-man tents. As I made my way across camp, picking my way by starlight over rocks and through clumps of sagebrush, I could hear the snores of men sleeping soundly in their cots, and the murmur of conversation and occasional laughter amongst die-hards playing cards by lamplight.

I climbed onto the truck, secured the latrine door behind me, and was preparing to do my business when the roar of an engine gunning to life brought me to my feet. As the truck ground into gear, I could hear whoops of laughter – obviously my presence hadn't gone unnoticed.

The truck lurched beneath me, and I grabbed for the door. Outside, a ring of soldiers hooted as the truck made a 360-degree loop around the site. But by the time I had reached the ground, my pranksters had cleared the area and sought cover.

Although I had my suspicions as to the ringleaders, I didn't object to being the brunt of an occasional joke, nor was I above distributing one myself, so I laughed it off. But I knew the guys would be waiting for me to retaliate, and as I stumbled across the darkened field toward my cot, I wondered how I would play my hand.

As dawn burst over the horizon in a watercolor haze of pink and gold, I joined the early birds as they stood smoking and drinking their morning coffee. And rolled my eyes when they snickered about their late-night prank.

A sudden rustle near the bushes at my feet drew my attention to a fat blow snake trying to make its retreat from the unwelcome commotion. Instinctively I reached down, plucked the harmless serpent from the ground and held it up for all to admire. I had once owned a boa constrictor, and as a child had spent many hours down by the lake with my friends catching water snakes and taking them home as pets.

Around me, men scattered in a flash of panic and all-out hysteria, and I knew what must be done.

With prize in hand, I marched across the clearing, stood before the half-opened flaps of the tent where my tormentors slept, and held out my offering. "Hey, guys," I said with a grin, "look what I found."

Within moments, as eyes focused and realization dawned, an array of soldiers stampeded for safety. Some wore shorts and tees as they fled from the tent. Others had trousers dangling from one leg as they hobbled for cover. And everywhere, dust and debris swirled as they knocked over cots, gear, and each other.

I had not expected such chaos, nor had I intended to bring so many men to the brink of heart failure. I had only wanted to prove that I could hold my own.

As I stood in the doorway watching all those battle-trained men fleeing for their lives, I felt a momentary stab of guilt.

Then I recalled that even Achilles had had his heel. And I laughed as I thought how a woman and a harmless little snake had just brought a tent full of soldiers to their knees.

Michele Hunter Mirabile
Army National Guard

# TWENTY-NINE

*"Lead me, follow me, or get out of my way."*
General George Patton, Jr.

Marine Science Technician Kira Johnson joined the Coast Guard directly out of high school. A former member of the Ceremonial Honor Guard, she now answers phones for the National Response Center, taking reports on everything from chemical spills to security breaches. At home, when she's not chasing after her toddler son, she likes to play the trumpet.

## DOING THE SAME JOB FOR THE SAME COUNTRY

I grew up in Las Vegas and did not want to spend the rest of my life there.

Because the Coast Guard was the only service no member of my family had yet joined, I decided to let the military pay for my education, and headed off for basic training two weeks after graduating from high school.

At boot camp, recruiters from the Ceremonial Honor Guard came and talked to my company. At the time, height requirements were over five feet, ten inches for females, and over six feet for men. At five feet, eleven inches, I was the only female in my company tall enough to qualify, so after basic, I headed off to TISCOM (Telecommunications and Information Systems Command) at Alexandria, Virginia, and began training for the opportunity to join the elite ranks of the Honor Guard.

Approximately seventy Coast Guard men and women make up the Honor Guard – except during inaugural season when those numbers go up. They represent the 38,000 men and women of this branch of service at funerals and parades in Washington D.C.

Although my training wound up on hold for a short time due to 9/11, it started up with vigor. In addition to maintaining our brass and uniforms, weapons manual and marching were daily practices during the workday, as well as after hours.

On normal days when we didn't have ceremonies or joint service training, we began at 0700 hours with some form of exercise, such as volleyball or a run. Afterward, we changed into our Trops uniform, which is a light-blue shirt with our HG badge if we had earned it, and our nametag. We also wore shirt stays, which were attached to the bottom of the seam of the shirt and the top of the socks.

Then we stood inspection. Shirts and pants had to be wrinkle-free, and have military creases and sharp peaks in the front. Each piece of brass had to be earned by several perfect uniforms, and had to be highly polished with no scratches or nicks.

When our uniform was deemed perfect, our clickers were earned and maintained for a certain period of time. Then we were able to wear them on our corofrems – patent leather/perma-shiny shoes with metal taps on the bottom and brass clickers on the inside heels. The soles were edge-dressed to be as shiny as the shoes themselves. Shorter members wore shorter shoes, meaning thicker soles. Mine were about four soles thick, called quads.

Finally we earned our breastplate, a large ceremonial belt buckle worn on a white belt.

Once all aspects of the Honor Guard were perfected, a trainee went through a going up ceremony. Following an inspection by the person in charge of the ceremony, the trainee marched in front of all HG soldiers and fellow trainees, performing all manuals and ceremonial sequences, while being given commands by the OIC, Chief, or NCO in charge.

As soon as all manuals and ceremonial sequences were finished, the soldier(s) were marched to the middle of the marching area and put at ceremonial at ease, to stand tight while the Honor Guard stared, talked, made fun of, or taunted them.

At this point, those in charge of the ceremony left the area to discuss whether or not the soldier would become part of the HG that day. In order for that to happen, minimal mistakes could be made.

When they all came back in, the HG formed up in a line, and a tense silent wait began. Either the phrase "rope 'em" which meant you were now part of the Honor Guard, or "fall out" which meant you failed, were shouted. If you were roped, you endured congratulations from the HG, all the while protecting that huge brass plate you spent hours on the night before from the soldiers who licked their fingers and tried to swipe them across it.

For ceremonies men and women wore the same uniform, which consisted of a dress jacket with large medals and a white rope or aiguillette over the shoulder, the HG badge if earned, and a white dress shirt and blue slacks. We also carried the 1902 bolt action Springfield rifle.

Because loose strands of hair were shaved from the back of our heads, and mine had been shaved almost halfway up, several times I got called "young man" or "sir." At first I took offense, and then I realized I did my job as well as the men I worked with and I felt proud of my image.

With training complete, I had to qualify for a number of duties which included firing party for funerals, shoulder guard for colors, body bearing, and flag folding. Shoulder guard and platoon were my main marching duties. We also stood watch once a week – twice a week if we were shorthanded due to ceremonies.

For the two and a half years I belonged to the Honor Guard, my duties ranged from working on photography at some ceremonies – mainly drill team jobs – to working in the flag locker pressing flags, replacing old flags and streamers, shining toppers for flag staffs, and bases for flags.

I also marched several ceremonies in the platoon including funerals, ceremonies at the Tomb of the Unknown Soldier, parades in Washington D.C. and Old Town, Virginia, and shoulder guard on some out-of-state ceremonies.

Arlington National Cemetery is one of the most amazing and emotional places I've ever seen. All those tombstones really put into perspective how many lives have been lost over the years to protect our rights, our liberties, and our way of life.

I also marched several ceremonies at the White House, and at one of those ceremonies President George W. Bush stopped, turned to my platoon and said, "Thank you." It was one of my proudest moments. In addition, I have met the previous Commandant of the Coast Guard, Admiral Loy, and the current Commandant, Admiral Collins, as well as the Deputy Secretary of Defense, and the Secretary of Defense.

At parades, the HG shows the precision and perfection of the military. Regardless of the weather, Americans come out to show their respect and support. They wave flags and stand as we pass. Though we cannot turn to look at faces as we march, I would often catch a glimpse of people crying. War veterans, who could barely walk or stand, struggled to rise from their wheelchairs to salute as a platoon passed. The feeling is indescribable. It is a feeling of complete and utter love of country that can only be generated by watching a parade or wearing a uniform.

I also played taps at "non-national" ceremonies. My most difficult ceremony was a funeral in which I played taps on my dad's old trumpet, about a week after the one-year anniversary of my great-grandmother's funeral. She had been my hero.

Being able to play taps myself evoked a whole new level of emotions toward the military, and I have never felt any of these stronger than I did on that day. Chills radiated over my flesh as I heard the sound of the trumpet and thought of my grandmother. I was overcome, and when I got back on the bus, I started to cry.

Funerals are a big part of the Honor Guard. We represent the branch of service to which the deceased family member belonged, with pride, respect, and dedication. Bodybearers carry the casket to the church or chapel, walk beside the caisson as it carries the soldier's body to the cemetery, and carry the casket to its final resting spot. They also fold the flag into a triangle, and deliver it to a family member with a speech and a salute.

Each branch has its own Ceremonial Honor Guard. The competition between services is actually quite amusing, especially with the men. You've heard all the nicknames: Army infantry are called ground pounders, Marines are bullet magnets and jarheads, the Navy are squids, the Coast Guard are puddle pirates, and the Air

Force are the "Army Air Corps" (mainly because they take offense to it) and the chair force because they are sometimes perceived by the other services to be lazy.

While each service brags they are the best, one thing I learned in the military is that each branch has to rely on each other for a lot of things.

We are all doing the same job, for the same country, and for similar reasons.

Petty Officer Kira Johnson
U.S. Coast Guard

# THIRTY

*"If a man does his best, what else is there?"*
General George Patton, Jr.

India Roderick joined the Coast Guard in 1990. During her nine-year enlistment, she married a coastie and was pregnant for every major move. She experienced many adventures, and served for nearly three years aboard the 270-foot cutter *Northland*. Currently, she is pursuing a degree in behavioral science.

## WHAT A RUSH!

One late afternoon, while on duty at Coast Guard Station Little Creek, Virginia, I was putting away tools and things in the boathouse when an emergency call came into the station and the siren sounded.

We ran toward the boats, and in moments the coxswain, two engineers, and myself as crewman, had launched a 41- foot utility boat commonly referred to as a search and rescue boat (SAR).

It was such an adrenaline rush!

As soon as the engines were started and the radio on, the station informed us an 80-foot trawler had lost power in Chesapeake Bay, and now drifted south across the shipping channel. A fire had engulfed the engine room, and three fishermen were on board. A trawler is a fishing boat with long arms and "birds" used to drag out the nets. The boat used in *The Perfect Storm* is a trawler, and the depiction of the coasties in that movie is very accurate.

As we approached the burning vessel in the open waters of the bay, the fishermen jumped overboard. Fortunately the sea conditions were pretty calm, just small waves with only a one-to two-foot roll.

We came up alongside them, with one of our engineers on the bow area telling the driver the distances of the hull to the survivors, and to the trawler. And our other engineer and I brought the fishermen on board one at a time. Though I am not a big woman nor overly strong for my size, I had plenty of strength that day and he expressed surprise at how much I helped in pulling the fishermen onto our boat.

Luckily the fishermen were not injured. They said they had jumped as soon as they saw us because they were nervous about the flames that raged in their engine room and the propane tanks sitting on the deck.

Because we needed to stay in our current position with the disabled and now unmanned trawler, we called back to the station and requested the secondary crew to come out in the 20-foot RHI and pick up the fishermen.

Using the water cannon mounted on the bow of our ship, we started shooting straight into the open deck hatch to the engine room of the trawler. One of our engineers manned the cannon for about twenty minutes, and then I took a turn. The heat coming off the boat was intense, and I felt like I was in an oven, or had a hair dryer blowing on my face and hands.

Although we were able to get the fire down to a moderate level, we still had to remain aware of the propane tanks on the deck, bolted to the side of the pilothouse. In addition, we were losing sunlight, the tide was going out, and the flow was taking the trawler toward the center span of the Chesapeake Bay Bridge.

We put our engineers on board the trawler to hook up the towline, staying in constant communication with the station, and we advised them to call the bridge police to inform them of a possible collision.

Ready for a fishing trip, the trawler was loaded down with ice and fuel, and very, very heavy. Even without all the water we had just pumped into the engine room, a boat of this size generally exceeded the towing range of our SAR.

The engineers reported the fire now smoldered, and the propane tanks were warm – but not too hot, thank God – and proceeded to hook up the eye of the towline I threw them. The boat drifted bow forward, the same way it would travel if the engines were working, and we knew it would be a bit of a slingshot action to pull the boat around and get her headed west.

Because the fire was still a very real threat and the engineers needed to remain on the disabled trawler, they moved to the aft corner of the port side of the pilothouse in order to avoid the propane tanks on the starboard side.

As we faced west, pulling with all we had, I stood on the deck, staying in communication with the driver, and keeping an eye on the towline. I had never been in a towing situation where we were in such direct danger, but the alternative meant allowing the trawler to crash into the busy bridge, resulting in a very real threat of death or serious injury to commuters crossing in their cars.

We had to make a wide turn, but we were running out of room and closing in on the bridge. We turned to the port and gradually brought up the power on the 41's engines. When the towline finally came under strain, it jumped out of the water and within a few moments popped and twisted under the immense pressure.

Quickly I went inside the cabin and closed the door. I could see the tow rope area from inside and had no desire to suffer from the snap back of the line if it parted. I had seen safety movies showing sailors being torn in half, or getting their thighs broken by snapped lines.

We had to get that trawler away from the bridge, and we needed the 82-foot ship based in Little Creek. Although we called the station and requested support, a ship of that size takes time to call in the crew and get underway, and in the meantime we had no other option but to make things work.

Now it was almost dark, and we could see the headlights of cars crossing the bridge. Although we weren't making much headway, at least we weren't going backward. After about an hour and a half straight of having the trawler under tow, our fuel had dropped to a quarter of a tank. But we couldn't let up the pressure on the trawler because the tide moved out faster now, making it a constant fight to just keep our station.

It seemed like it took forever for the trawler to turn, and when she finally did the engineers were close enough to the bridge that they could see the make and color of passing cars. Later they told us they had already decided the right moment to jump from the trawler before it hit the bridge.

Forty minutes after we had requested help, we received news that our 82-foot ship was coming out of the channel to take over. What a relief!

They hooked up their towline before we let up the pressure, using a different rig that made it capable of allowing them to take the tow under pressure while we released our line.

We collected the engineers from the trawler and went back to the station, exhausted and exhilarated – which was good, because we still had to make sure the boat was ready to go out again if another alarm sounded in the night.

I helped with the chores of replacing the towline, and the proper inspection of the one we had just maxed out. And the engineers had to do a good deal of work in the engine room, because the engines had strained unchecked for so long.

Later we received the Commandants Letter of Accommodation, which is ranked up there pretty high on the scale of uniform ribbons, as well as a team award.

Of all the ribbons I ever earned, I was most proud of these. Although we had drilled and practiced many times in preparation for such an event, we had physically rescued three fishermen from the water, and prevented countless loss of life on the bridge by averting a collision with a disabled and burning boat.

Despite the dangerous and difficult job, we had worked great as a team and no one had been injured or lost.

It was also the kind of thing I had dreamed of doing when I had initially committed my life to the military.

What a rush!

India Roderick
U.S. Coast Guard

# THIRTY-ONE

*"History does not long entrust the care of freedom*
*to the weak or the timid."*
General Dwight D. Eisenhower

While stationed in New Orleans with the Marine Corps in 2005, Lance Corporal Heather Weiss became engaged to her husband, Daniel, and experienced first-hand the destruction and chaos of one of our country's most cataclysmic hurricanes.

## CALM IN THE MIDST OF A STORM

Just as New Orleans' levies crumbled in the face of Hurricane Katrina, so did all my dreams and meticulous preparations, as I became an evacuee only days before my wedding.

Daniel and I met while serving with the Marine Corps in New Orleans, and we had planned to exchange nuptials at the Presidential Palace on September 9, 2005. I wanted everything to be perfect, from our engagement on Valentine's Day to the hand-made favors now floating somewhere in the Gulf of Mexico as alligator bait.

On the afternoon of August 28, while Daniel was still in Japan completing his tour, I grabbed only what I could stuff into a duffel bag and escaped the approaching storm with four of my Marine Corps friends. We made our way to Baton Rouge, through streets jammed with traffic and panicking crowds, where we were lucky enough to find shelter at a motel.

The next day, we traveled on to the Trail Dust Inn in Sulphur Springs, Texas. At the lowest point in my life, I called my family in Michigan and Arizona, to tell them there wouldn't be a wedding in New Orleans.

Although my plight paled against the immensity of the disaster, as I began canceling and postponing a host of details, word of my predicament spread throughout the community. Wedding planners and volunteers came forward, and offers for everything from flowers to a horse-drawn carriage began pouring in.

Many wonderful people put their heads together and vowed to make our wedding one to remember, Sulphur Springs style. They couldn't bring back the dead or rebuild a city, but they were determined to give a displaced bride the wedding of her dreams.

The justice of the peace assured me all legal work could be done in Hopkins County. So, marriage licenses were obtained, the fees to change Daniel's ticket were taken care of, and my family and friends were contacted and informed of the new wedding location in Heritage Hall.

Despite the chaos and devastation of a hurricane, Daniel and I were married on Friday, September 9, after all.

I can't thank the people of Sulphur Springs enough for their generosity and graciousness. Because of their efforts, we enjoyed a storybook wedding complete with perfect weather, arrangements and festivities.

It was like a moment of calm in the midst of a storm, and a reminder that life goes on despite hardship and tragedy.

Lance Corporal Heather Weiss
U.S. Marine Corps

# THIRTY-TWO

*"The truth of the matter is that you always know the right thing to do. The hard part is doing it."*
Norman Schwarzkopf

Staff Sergeant Jaclyn Long joined the Army right out of high school, and served from 1996 – 2001. Today she is a member of the Utah Army National Guard's 211th Aviation Battalion, and works full-time as Aviation Retention NCO. She enjoys baseball, and coaching her son's T-ball team.

## DIRECT FROM AFGHANISTAN

My husband and I are both members of the 211th Aviation Battalion. When our unit was deployed in 2004, my husband went with them to Afghanistan, and I stayed home to care for our two children.

Near the end of his deployment, my husband told me a couple of women from his unit had found two dogs running wild, and rescued them from being used as target practice by locals. "They've raised enough money to bring them back to the States," he said, "but it looks like the dogs will beat us home. Do you think we could help out by keeping them for a while?"

I thought how hard could it be? I already had two kids, a dog and a cat. I love dogs, and since it would only be for a short while, I agreed to take care of them until the battalion returned.

About five weeks later I got an e-mail from one of the women who had found the dogs, telling me they were ready to be picked up.

It was really going to happen. I was even further surprised when I saw them. I had thought they would be some crazy-looking dogs coming from afar, but they were cute lovable puppies with soft, white fur.

When I knelt down to pet them, Chopper, the playful little male jumped on me and knocked me on my butt. And of course, his sister, Apache, had to join in the fun by tackling my face and licking me nonstop.

We put the puppies in the truck – thank heaven for extended cabs – kids in the back, dogs in the front with me. Apache loved the ride home, but Chopper didn't take to it so kindly. And nobody had bothered to warn me they got carsick.

When I pulled into my driveway and wrestled the kids out of the back seat, the puppies weren't in a hurry to go anywhere. They were too busy puking up their whole lunch. There were dog-food chunks everywhere – on the seats, between the seats, on their feet, and all over their leashes.

I cleaned them up and took them in the house, where they busied themselves playing with the kids and exploring every aspect of this foreign place. It didn't take long for them to wear themselves out.

Needless to say, the kids fell in love with these puppies that had taken over the house and were soon sleeping on our beds.

Chopper was playful all of the time. And Apache soaked up attention by rolling onto her back and waiting for someone to pet her stomach, even if no one looked her way.

Our other dog, Smokey, seemed to be in heaven as well. He loved his new playmates and the three of them would eat anything and everything in sight. They roamed the backyard eating hoses, toys, sticks, and rocks. Nothing seemed to be off limits.

As time went by, I actually forgot my job was to take care of these dogs on a temporary basis. They had become part of our family, and I refused to think about giving them up.

In April 2005 my husband returned from Afghanistan, and when he discovered the dogs were sleeping on our beds, that practice came to a sudden halt. Now they were only allowed inside during the day, although I occasionally sneaked them in. "It's just one night," I would tell him.

By now my children had become so attached to these adorable hyper dogs that I knew they would be heartbroken to lose them. So I made a decision – we would keep them.

At first we were all happy with this turn of events. But soon Apache started barking every time the wind blew, or every three minutes – whichever came first.

As a result of this nightly disturbance we decided we couldn't keep Apache after all, and another member of our unit quickly adopted her. It was a sad day to see this wonderful puppy leave our home, but she is now the ruler of a new home. And yes, she has children to play with, and gets to sleep inside on their beds.

As the newest member of our family, Chopper keeps us on our toes. In addition to keeping our dog and our children company, he has learned to fetch, sit, shake, and . . . well, that's about it.

He has also learned a fence is his wall to the outside world and with a little effort he can get out.

On one of his excursions, he reverted to his native ways and chased a neighbor's goats. When he killed one and wounded another, I thought it was the end of the road for Chopper. I figured he was about to be a goner.

To our surprise, however, everything worked out well. We paid for the vet bills, increasing the value of the now-healed goat by $725.00. And Chopper has a better understanding of a fence – thanks to some training with a shock collar.

Life is full of challenges, and we all have to deal with them as best we can.

However Chopper tends to bring on some good ones and I don't think we have seen the end of them yet!

But we love him. Not only is he a constant reminder of the service our unit rendered in Afghanistan, he is a prime example that while any dog can be placed in a home, only a very special dog can make a family whole.

Staff Sergeant Jaclyn Long
Army National Guard

# THIRTY-THREE

*"I learned that good judgement comes from experience
and that experience grows out of mistakes."*
General H. Norman Schwarzkopf

In 2001, Marine Science Technician Kira Johnson joined the
Coast Guard directly out of high school. A former member of the
Ceremonial Honor Guard, she now answers phones for the National
Response Center, taking reports on everything from chemical spills
to security breaches. At home, when she's not chasing after her
toddler son, she likes to play the trumpet.

## SWEET REVENGE

One day, I stood watch in the barracks at TISCOM
(Telecommunications and Information Systems Command) with
another member of the Coast Guard Honor Guard who had become
known as a slacker and a troublemaker. A know-it-all, he always
showed up late for duty, and seldom did anything required.

As a watchstander, our duties were to stand gate watch –
which meant checking all identification before allowing people to

enter through the gate – and make sure proper respects were paid to officers.

My responsibilities, while in charge of the watch, were to make sure cleanups were completed, shifts began on time, and problems between personnel got resolved. Although I didn't have to assist with the cleaning, I always tried to lend a hand because I knew it was a bummer to be lower on the Honor Guard chain.

In keeping with his reputation, this guy refused to help with anything throughout the day, and by the end of our shift I was pretty fed up with him and his constant slacking.

Around midnight, just after our so-called slacker had gone to bed exhausted from his day of shirking duties and his evening out, a bunch of us decided it was time to teach him a lesson and exact some revenge for the frustration he caused us.

After some careful plotting, we strung packing tape across the outside of his door, attached a bullhorn to an alarm clock set to go off within the next couple of minutes, and lowered it through the ceiling above his head. Acoustic tiles made it easy for us to pass things from one room to another.

When the alarm went off, I spoke loudly through the door, struggling to keep my voice steady as I told him he was late for watch.

"Oh, shit!" he said. "You're lying!"

I couldn't keep a straight face, but I stuck to my story, telling him he had the 0400-0800 watch.

It took some persuasion, but finally he said, "Okay, Okay, I'm up! I'm coming!"

As soon as I knew he was up, I hurried out of sight, trying not to laugh out loud.

A few minutes later, confused and half-asleep, he flung open the door and got caught in the tape with his shirt unbuttoned, pants zipped halfway, and obviously still feeling the effects of his night out.

Wild-eyed and casting about for someone to blame, he wrestled free, then stumbled into the hall and down the stairs with his boots unlaced and falling off.

We all followed him to the quarterdeck, and started laughing hysterically when the watchstander asked if he was all right.

"You guys suck!" said our slacker when he came upstairs, glaring as he stomped past us toward his room. After all, a slacker is a slacker, and all the excitement of our big joke wasn't going to keep him from going right back to bed.

We just stood there, laughing so hard we were almost in tears.

Though I can't say for sure whether or not we gave him enough motivation to improve his work habits, I can say he kept a careful "watch" on the rest of us for some time afterward.

Petty Officer Kira Johnson
U.S. Coast Guard

# THIRTY-FOUR

*"The mothers and fathers of America will give you their sons
and daughters . . . with the confidence in you that you will not
needlessly waste their lives. And you dare not. That's the burden
the mantle of leadership places upon you. You could be the person
who gives the orders that brings about the deaths of thousands
and thousands of young men and women. It is an awesome
responsibility. You cannot fail. You dare not fail . . . "*
General H. Norman Schwarzkopf

In 1977, Colonel Linda P. Higgins enlisted in the Army National
Guard. She was the first female in the state of Utah to become a non-
medical commissioned officer, and to wear a maternity uniform. In
her twenty-eight years of service, she has held six commands, and
enjoyed a career filled with memorable people and experiences.

## THE MOST FUN YOU CAN HAVE

When I worked in the office of the Secretary of State, my
boss announced he wouldn't run for office after all and I knew I

would lose my job. So I put in for a transfer and said I would take anything with compatible pay.

Because I worked specifically with the attorney general's office, when I received a call saying an administrative position was available for the adjutant general, I thought they said attorney general. Therefore, I interviewed at the Utah National Guard Armory, and was hired as a civilian state employee.

Shortly afterward, a good friend of mine invited me to go out to Camp Williams to watch her boyfriend, who was in the 19th Special Forces Group, do a parachute demonstration. I knew then I wanted to jump. I had been impressed by the quality of people I had met in the Guard, so I signed up and went to jump school.

Upon graduation, I figured I could get through just about anything after what I had experienced, so I decided to go to Officer Candidate School, where I spent the next sixteen months training at Camp Williams to become a second lieutenant.

When I received my commission, I was assigned to go back to Camp Williams to the Utah Military Academy. For the first time in Utah's history, females were attending the school, and they wanted a female tactical officer to be there.

About a year later, I went to State Headquarters. Because it was 1977 and no one really quite knew what to do with women, and since no one had particularly mentored me, I had selected an adjutant general (AG) branch on the recommendation of others. But when I went to the colonel and asked him what kind of unit I could command someday, he looked at me like I was from Mars. "Well," he said, "you are AG branch, and AG Corps doesn't command – not in Utah anyway. We aren't structured for that."

So I sought the advice of my good friend, a personnel officer who knew just about every regulation ever written, and told him I wanted to re-branch so I could be a commander, and he showed me how to do it. Apparently it was not a common practice, but I did it, and I went back to that same colonel and said, "Now, show me your chart and tell me what unit I can command."

He tried to steer me toward medical, but I didn't want that route. I selected ordinance, and the colonel said, "Well, there's this little maintenance company, and technically a woman could command that."

I interviewed with the commander of that company and got on as the executive officer. But the NCO I had to work with turned out to be the most ornery sergeant first class I had ever met in my life. At first he didn't want to deal with me. I thought he was anti-female, but I soon learned he was really shy and simply didn't know how to act. He was nervous about the men's behavior and their language around me, and when I wasn't in the room he would chew them out.

One day I called him into my office. "Here's the deal," I said. "I am a stupid lieutenant. I know nothing, but I'm willing to learn. However, I'm *your* lieutenant. So you can either make me a good one, or ignore me and we'll just get along until I find a new position. But my goal is to command this unit someday. So you can either have a good commander, or a crappy lieutenant. Take your pick."

He decided the wise choice was to mentor me. He took me under his wing and taught me a lot of things, including the fact that a good NCO is the most valuable tool an officer can have to work with. Since that day, I have valued the NCO Corps and what they can do, because they really are where the rubber meets the road when it comes to getting things done. Despite our rocky beginning, meeting him was one of the most influential experiences of my career. A perfectionist, he believed in working hard, and will forever be one of my favorite NCOs.

On my first trip to the field with this company, we set up shop in the usual big clamshell trailer. In the field, a maintenance company sets up in about a five-mile cluster, and as the shop office, ours was the first trailer a customer would approach in a forward area.

As nighttime fell, everyone started putting their bunks together in this trailer, and when I walked in, my sergeant said, "Gosh, I didn't think about it. Where are you going to sleep?"

"Right here in the trailer."

"You can't do that," he said.

"Yes I can. And I will. We'll all have our PT uniforms on, and I don't expect anyone to be inappropriate."

This was before co-ed even existed, and I know it was a really hard transition for him and the other guys to come to terms with, but it all worked out, and we all got along in the end.

About a year later, our commander moved on to another position and I took his place. Having a company command is probably the most fun you can have in the military because you get to be in charge – for good or bad. You get the credit for all the good stuff your people do, and you also take it in the rear when things go bad.

There are very few things in the government you can step back from and measure progress, but as a commander with a good first sergeant, you really can influence the way a unit trains and succeeds.

I got to know my soldiers. I knew who was in love, and who was going through a divorce. We were like family, because unlike active duty soldiers we didn't move on every two years. Some members of that unit had been there for over twenty years.

While with the 115th, I became the first non-medical female commissioned officer in the Utah National Guard. I also became the first woman in Utah to wear a maternity uniform. When the Army first came out with this style, I went to Fort Ord, California, to get one, and I'm sure it was a trial for all those tough, gruff maintenance guys to see their commander wearing a maternity smock.

The first time I wore it into the building a woman came up to me and asked, "What kind of uniform is that?"

"Maternity," I said.

"What organization do you belong to?"

"The Army National Guard."

"You mean you can be in the Army and be pregnant?" she asked.

At this time, pregnant women had the option to either stay in or get out. But the whole concept was still beyond some people's imagination, and I often had to explain that just because a woman was pregnant didn't mean she lost her capacity to think, or her ability to perform her required duties.

When I left the maintenance company, I went to the Training Site as logistics officer for Camp Williams, where I got to run the Troop Issue Subsistence Area, which is where all the units come to get their food for the weekend drills. I also ran the fuel and ammo dumps.

From there, I went on to STARC (State Headquarters Area Command) as executive officer, where things were more relaxed. When I started writing training schedules I realized it was a step they hadn't yet taken, and it was kind of fun to watch the learning process. But I finally convinced those in charge that State Headquarters should set the example above all units, and if they were going to put out policy, they had better be doing it themselves. It changed the way they did business, although I had to drag some of them into that century.

Not long afterward, I became STARC Commander and received a promotion to major. This was a unique position because not only was I responsible for the soldiers, but my staff consisted of about nine colonels who all thought they were my boss, even though I answered to the Chief of Staff and the Deputy General.

I learned how to be very tactful, and that the best way to get what I wanted was to go to each one of them personally, convince them it was their idea, and try to make them part of the decision-making process.

Then I would I go to the Chief of Staff and tell him I'd like to do things a certain way, and he would go directly to staff meeting and talk to all those colonels who had already bought off on it. In other words, I learned how to be politically correct, which is a valuable survival skill in the military.

My next assignment was taking on the 128th Mobile Public Affairs Unit.

At that time, the 6th Army was looking to re-evaluate how public affairs units were divided among the U.S., a situation that threatened the 128th organizationally. My job was to help them do their training and get caught up on the military side of things. They were good journalists, but they didn't possess required soldier skills.

About a year and a half later, I received the opportunity to go out to the Regional Training Institute at Camp Williams and take a lieutenant colonel slot. It was quite a privilege. But I feared the 128th would be deployed to Bosnia, and I didn't think it was fair that

I wouldn't get to go with them after all the work I'd done pushing them through all the holes to get prepared. So I asked the general if they did get called up, if he would let me go back to that unit.

In October I transferred to Camp Williams. And on Thanksgiving weekend, the National Guard Bureau called me at home to tell me the Public Affairs Unit was going to be called up. Because they didn't have an updated alert roster, they were under the impression I was still the commander. So I called the general, and about a day and a half later he called me back and told me the current commander had asked me to return to the unit, as he was not comfortable deploying with only two months under his belt.

Of course I agreed, since I had begged for this position. And I had already told my very supportive family this was what I wanted to do if I had the opportunity.

As it turned out, we were called up and deployed to Bosnia from January 1995 – August 1996, where we were stationed at USAREUR (United States Army Europe & 7th Army), Germany, and then split up for assignments from there. I had teams in Croatia, Bosnia, Sardinia, and Germany. It was an amazing experience. Because I had requirements that allowed me to spend time with each of these elements, I basically spent nine months all over Europe visiting with these soldiers.

As a mobile public affairs unit, our mission varied. We escorted a lot of media, such as *Newsweek,* CNN, or anyone else who wanted to come over and visit the troops or investigate the goings-on. In fact, Princess Diana spent a lot of time in Bosnia. Although I didn't get to meet her she was often in the area. Also, we escorted dignitaries, and I even met the Secretary of the Army, William Cohen.

As one of our duties, we produced and wrote the stories for a show called *Good Morning USAREUR* for the Armed Forces Network in Europe. My soldiers did all the videotaping, editing, and broadcasting.

In addition, I had a whole team that came in every morning to screen newspapers in Heidelberg, Germany, for the commander in Chief at USAREUR. We contracted with newspaper agencies to send a gentleman to deliver all the publications to us that were scheduled to go out to the public that day. As a result, we'd see them two hours before they hit the street, and we'd go through every article, highlighting any potential stories of interest, things that might come up during the day, or questions the media might ask.

By eight every morning, this team sent a runner to the general's aide to deliver a stack of three by five cards, with the answers to all the issues we had gathered the statistics for and done the homework and research on, written on the other side.

As a result, the general carried a stack of cards with him every day, so if he were approached in a meeting or on the street, or in any environment whatsoever, he had at his fingertips all the facts – whether or not they were controversial.

*60 Minutes* also came over to interview our general, and we got to help prepare him for that, and get a first-hand look at what goes on behind the scenes.

I was gone for nearly a year, and leaving my children was probably the hardest thing I've ever done. But anytime I started feeling sorry for myself, all I had to do was look around and see the thousands of other moms and dads there with me, and to realize that they, too, missed their families.

A wonderful thing did come from my deployment, however, as my husband was forced to bond and interact with my son who suffers from a disability, and to go through therapy with him in order to strengthen their relationship.

Upon my return to Utah, I went back to my assignment with the Regional Training Institute. When the commander of the regiment was selected to make general, I decided it was time for me to retire. But he called me in and asked me not to retire just yet. I figured he wanted me to train his replacement and help the new guy. Instead, I could have been knocked over with a feather when I received a call telling me I would be the new regimental commander.

Never in a thousand years had I dreamed I would make full-bird colonel, let alone be the first female in Utah to make O-6 as a commissioned officer.

About this time, another woman was promoted to command sergeant major, making her the first female in the Utah National Guard of that rank, and I got to pin her. I also got to escort Lieutenant Governor Olene Walker to the stage to become Utah's first female governor.

In my twenty-eight years of service, I have had six commands, and an amazing career filled with fascinating people and memorable experiences.

I had the unforgettable opportunity to visit Arlington, Virginia, to see those rows upon rows of headstones marking soldiers who had given their lives for my freedom. It was an emotional experience, as was the time I stood with my family on the shores of Normandy.

But my proudest moment occurred at Pearl Harbor, while viewing the actual footage of that event. As I looked down the row at my children and saw tears rolling down their cheeks, I knew they

truly understood why I do what I do. And why their father, who is also
in the military, does what he does.

Colonel Linda P. Higgins
Army National Guard

# THIRTY-FIVE

*"With malice toward none, with charity for all, with firmness in the*
*right, as God gives us to see the right, let us strive on to finish the*
*world we are in, to bind up the nation's wounds."*
Abraham Lincoln

In 1942, Vivian E. Dimke Bellemere joined the Army Air Corps as a member of the 349th Air Evacuation Group. A year later, she graduated with the first Flight Nurses Training class. After her discharge in 1945, she proceeded to support her husband in his service career, and accompany him on his many U.S. assignments.

## GOOD MORNING, MOTHER

I trained as a nurse in St. Joseph's hospital, near my hometown of Clarkston, Washington. Although it wasn't a large, prestigious city, I received excellent training with an emphasis on things like bedside manners.

In 1939, while working as a nurse at Swedish Hospital in Seattle, the chief nurse and I went to the pier to watch the ships come in. We saw a Japanese ship, marked with the telltale red circle, come into the harbor to get scrap iron. The nurse said, "We will be getting that scrap iron back someday."

On December 7, 1941, the Japanese bombed Pearl Harbor. At this time I worked at the Veterans Hospital in San Francisco. Threatened by Japanese planes going up and down the coast of Northern California, the hospital was evacuated to Fort Whipple Veterans Hospital, in Prescott, Arizona.

I heard many of the older nurses say, "If I were younger, I'd join the service." This inspired me to sign up as a second lieutenant with the Army Air Corps at Albuquerque, New Mexico.

In 1942, Jimmy Stewart was stationed at Albuquerque as well. It was not uncommon for celebrities to join the war effort. One night he was at the Officers' Club while I was there with my escort, David Bellemere, whom I had met at Kirtland Air Force Base, along with a mutual friend of ours who was a Catholic priest.

The priest led us over to meet Jimmy, by making a path through the crowd of officers' wives surrounding him. "Make way!" he said. "Make way for a nurse!"

Jimmy smiled at me and said, "That's a nice uniform you're wearing."

Assigned to the 349th Air Evacuation Group, I attended Flight Nurses Training with the Army Air Forces in Bowman Field, Kentucky. I was in the first class to graduate on February 18, 1943.

While I was there, David Bellemere proposed to me over the telephone. A short time later he came to visit. We were both scared, because of the war and the uncertainty of our futures, and I said, "Marry me now or never."

Soon after we were married, David was sent overseas to war for eighteen months. He was a B-29 pilot. At this time, the Army Air Corps pushed out pilots at a frequent rate. They were known as the ninety-day wonders. And if they were really sharp, they became fighter pilots.

For a solid year we flight nurses were not given an assignment, so I requested a transfer to a station hospital.

As a WWII nurse, the main difficulty was seeing so many wounded men and not knowing initially whether they were dead or alive. But my aim was to do something to make a personal connection. So I always tried to fluff a pillow, hold his hand, or tell a joke. Unfortunately, a number of nurses hadn't developed good bedside manners, nor did they make much of an effort to ease the patients.

Right from the beginning, however, I tried so hard to make them comfortable that if they didn't laugh at my jokes, I came to feel as though I had failed them miserably.

I tried to give each one of my patients special attention. One young soldier's hands were bleeding from dermatitis. I asked the doctor if he thought sunlight would help. He said, "You can try."

As an experiment, I exposed the patient's hands to sunlight, increasing the amount each day. I'm not certain if that treatment was beneficial, but his dermatitis cleared up. In appreciation, he made me a large, beautiful copper tray with my name on it, which I still have and treasure to this day.

Although I had hoped to be deployed overseas as an air evacuation nurse, the waiting time in the U.S. hospitals, as well as the difficulty in rank advancement soon took a toll on my service interests.

When David came back from overseas in February 1945, I went to the Re-distribution Center in Santa Monica, California to meet him. Shortly after, I realized I was pregnant, and a lab test proved it to be true.

However, the station hospital where I worked wouldn't accept that lab test and did a test of its own. While walking down the hall to find out my pregnancy results, I met the lab technician.

He said, "Good morning, mother."

This was my discharge from the Army Air Corps in 1945.

Vivian E. Dimke Bellemere
Army Air Corps

# THIRTY-SIX

*"We will not tire, we will not falter, we will not fail."*
President George W. Bush

First Sergeant Patricia Diane Flores served in the Army from 1980 to 2004. Her military achievements include many firsts, including the first female on a Patriot Missile crew, and the first female Sergeant Major of the 10th Regiment Advanced ROTC Camp at Syracuse University.

## SERVING IN THE WORLD'S MOST OUTSTANDING ARMY

When three of my brothers went into the military – one in the Air Force, another in the Marine Corps, and yet another in the Army – I made up my mind that one day I would follow in their footsteps.

At the age of twenty-four, I decided to take the entry exam for the Army. Though I passed with flying colors, I determined it wasn't my time just yet.

A year later I decided to try again, but my test had expired and I had to repeat the entire process. Again, I passed with flying colors, so I figured it was time to get out of Pennsylvania and see the world. My father was very upset, and didn't want me to go. He didn't think the Army was a good place for women, and he was scared for me.

On February 17, 1980, I headed off to Fort Bliss, Texas, for basic training and advanced individual training. I specialized in Air Defense Artillery, and when training was complete, I went on to Germany where I spent the next several years. I truly enjoyed being there, learning about their culture, currency, and language.

When I left Germany, I worked as a reenlistment NCO at Fort Bliss, because my job was being closed out for another system coming on board. Females could not participate in this new system, and Congress still debated whether or not to let women train on it at all, not because it was hard, but because it would be a combat support system and females were not yet allowed in combat.

We were offered some very good jobs, but being the Air Defender that I was, I decided to wait it out because I knew sooner or later Congress would change that ruling. And sure enough, several years later, I became the first female to join the ranks of the Patriot System Air Defenders (16T crewmember). I was so proud.

As crewmembers we had to become certified, and we would train for weeks at a time. Because there were now women in the ranks, commanders and first sergeants had some decisions to make regarding showers, sleeping arrangements, and privacy.

Policies allowed women to have showers every twenty-four to forty-eight hours. Because we were housed in the same tents as the men, and we had more male soldiers than females, the men would leave for about a half-hour, and then the women would go for an hour.

A lot of men complained, saying they thought women were trying to get out of work and training by using their monthly period – or "girlfriend" as I call it – as an excuse. This became a concern for all commanders and first sergeants. But I never let the fact that I was a woman get in the way of doing my job. I had waited a long time to get that job, and I intended to keep it.

I knew there would be problems, however, because some of the women coming into this area of expertise were very soft. There were times when we were dirty, muddy, and smelled pretty bad because we would be moving from point A to point B and miss shower runs. Personally, I didn't care whether or not I could shower. I was a soldier, and I would wash up using my helmet and baby wipes.

But we made it through training, and soon we were packing up to go to Germany.

As section chief, I had seven soldiers working for me, and we trained and trained. With our first exercise we finished as top crew, and finally, I was promoted to staff sergeant in January 1989. Getting promoted had been difficult for me, as well as for other females, and it didn't seem to matter how hard we worked. In addition, every time the Army had said, "We need you here," I had packed up and gone – with or without my family.

In 1991, I was back in Fort Bliss, working as a platoon sergeant with an Air Defense unit. We were preparing to start field training when we received orders to deploy to Southwest Asia for Desert Storm. It was hard to leave my family, but they knew this was my job and I had to go.

I left with my unit in October 1992, and headed out to King Kahlid Military City, in Saudi Arabia (KKMC SWA), where we set up and trained. We lived in trailers, and our showers were in trailers as well. Although native women weren't allowed to drive or show any parts of their body, as female soldiers we did drive, as long as we kept our hair up and our headgear on.

We lived in our uniforms, which was not a problem. And when we were able to leave the compound, we were always with male soldiers. I would see women wearing black coverings from head to toe, and I always wished they could enjoy the same freedoms we did.

In Bahrain, however, the lifestyle appeared totally different. Women danced, smoked, and partied just like everyone else – alcohol and all.

When I made morale calls home, I would speak to my husband first and then to my son. It was so good to hear his voice. "Please come home, Mom," he would say, "all Dad ever cooks is potatoes and rice."

I missed him so much. But I would laugh, and tell him he had made my day.

In April of 1993, I left SWA and headed back to Fort Bliss, where I received another promotion, and became an instructor for the NCO Academy. Although I enjoyed my time there, and I have always enjoyed working with people from different backgrounds, the Commandant of the Academy was not very keen on females.

When the men received permanent change of stations he gave them high awards, but when I left he gave me a low one, even though I had graduated all of my students, and was the first instructor to have German students to graduate from the academy. I think this was the first time in my career I ever felt discriminated against.

161

But it didn't matter, because as my mother used to say, "What goes around comes around."

Several years later, I received orders to Syracuse University as Senior NCO of the ROTC. My first year there we received 198 inches of snow. I had never seen so much snow before in my life. Here, I experienced my second bout of discrimination, with a captain who had never been in a unit with a female. He would go around saying untrue things about me, but when confronted, he didn't have an explanation. I understood that the military consists of all kinds of people from different backgrounds, and we depend on each other to get the job done. But he just didn't get it.

I was selected as Sergeant Major of the 10th Regiment at the Camp, in July 2001, making me the first female Sergeant Major of the Advanced Camp ever. That was a very proud moment for me, as the Camp had been in existence for more than eighty years.

On March 1, 2004, I retired from the Army with twenty-four years of active service. Not all soldiers I met along the way were of good nature, and I wish I had been able to spend more time with my family, because I missed a lot of things such as birthdays, anniversaries, Valentine's Day and Christmas. But overall, my experience was great.

I loved being a soldier, and I feel blessed to have spent so many years in the service of the world's most outstanding Army.

First Sergeant Patricia Diane Flores, (retired)
U.S. Army

# THIRTY-SEVEN

*"Accept the challenges so that you can feel the exhilaration of victory."*
General George Patton, Jr.

India Roderick joined the Coast Guard in 1990. During her nine-year enlistment, she married a coastie and was pregnant for every major move. She experienced many adventures, and served for nearly three years aboard the 270-foot cutter *Northland.* Currently, she is pursuing a degree in behavioral science.

## A REAL CLIFFHANGER

One bright sunny day, while serving with the Coast Guard on board the Cutter *Northland,* we were docked in GITMO, or Guantanamo Bay, Cuba, and those of us not on duty had a beach party.

The lagoon at Cable Beach is about the size of a little league baseball field, enclosed by a rock reef, and perfect for swimming.

The area was also home to a group of large iguanas that loved Doritos. Having been exposed to all the military personnel that came here to visit and relax, they had developed a taste for junk food. Although they weren't pushy like dogs, if you approached their area and offered them a snack they would gratefully take it and wait for more.

Curious about what lay around the corner of the beach, I walked over to the eastern edge and stepped over the border to see even more rocks, including a beautiful low-lying formation, and a few dozen little caves on the ground. Although they were the perfect size for lizards, when high tide came in they would all be under water.

As I came around the corner, I ran into Jones and Jolley – a couple of guys from the ship. Because we all wanted to explore further, we decided it best to stick together. The beach, so blue and pristine, looked exactly the same as I had always imagined *Gilligan's Island*.

About an hour and a half later, as we made our way east along the coastline, the three of us ran into two more of our shipmates – Haldeman and Lieutenant B. Although the five of us were an unlikely group, we continued on together.

We had a wonderful time exploring nature and formations, and we enjoyed ourselves so thoroughly that when we reached a point of impasse, we noticed the sun had started to get low in the sky, and we didn't know where we were.

In front of us, a sheer cliff jutted out into the ocean. With the tide now coming in, it would be suicide to go around it at beach level. We had been traveling along the base of a steep rocky formation, and we needed to get to the top of it.

Spotting a crevice that went all the way up, I suggested we climb right there.

"Are you out of your mind?" Haldeman shook his head. The men all agreed it would be safer, smarter and easier to backtrack a bit to find another way up.

But I knew I could make it up the crevice, and if they didn't feel comfortable about climbing it, I didn't intend to ask them to try. Besides, I wasn't attempting to prove anything; I only wanted to do it for my own personal satisfaction.

The guys headed back, and I waited for a minute and then went for the crevice.

At first it was as easy as I had expected – not as easy as climbing steps by far, but very manageable. But by the time I had made it about halfway up – the distance of about a three-story building – I became acutely aware of the blowing wind and the crashing waves, and I started to get really nervous.

"Ya know," I said to myself, "maybe they were right after all." I decided to go back down the crevice and try to find the route the men had taken. But when I looked down, Lieutenant B. was in the process of climbing up. Now I had to get to the top, and I had to do it without knocking rocks down on his head.

The closer I got, however, the harder it was to find hand and footholds I could reach. Being only five feet, five inches tall, my options were certainly more limited than Lieutenant B.'s who stood easily six feet, two inches.

I made my way to the very last grapple before I reached the top. But no one was there to give me a hand – the other guys had not yet made it around. Below, the waves seemed to taunt me as they pounded on the rocks, and my heart thumped so loud it almost overpowered the sound of the ocean.

Terrified, my stomach flipped, and my arms and legs trembled.

Finally I just reached out a sweaty hand, grabbed a clump of dirt and grass and slid myself up onto the flat ground. As I lay there safe at last, staring up at the sky, I said, "Thank you, God. Thank you, God. Thank you, God."

Lieutenant B. still made his way up the crevice. I crawled to the edge and looked down on him. "How ya doin', sir?"

"Just fine," he said, but his face reflected the same anxiety I had felt while standing in that exact mid-way spot. "You make it okay?" he asked.

"Yes, sir. Just fine. I'll wait here for you."

"I'll be right there."

I could hear the tension in his voice, and I was scared to death for him. I knew what I had just gone through. If anything happened to him I would feel so responsible, even though I had in no way asked or challenged him to follow. He had made his own choice just as I had done mine. But I still felt a heavy burden of accountability for Lieutenant B.'s current position.

Haldeman, Jones, and Jolley joined me from another direction. They got there just before Lieutenant B. reached the threshold spot that had terrified me earlier. I could tell he was genuinely and deeply scared. He wasn't crying, whining or anything outward. But he sweat bullets, and had a wild-eyed expression as he searched for the final handholds. "How did you do this, India?" he asked. "What did you hold on to?" "I just reached out and got a clump of dirt and grass, and belly-crawled up here."

"No, not good enough. I need something better."

Jolley and I anchored Jones and Haldeman down as they got on their bellies and reached out for each of Lieutenant B.'s hands. But before he put his weight and trust into their hands – literally – he said, "I have a wife and two boys to go home to. Don't let go."

166

Again, my heart pounded in my eardrums. All of us shared in the feeling of fear and tension.

Three seconds later we all lay safely on the ground laughing in relief.

As it turned out, we came up on the plateau next to a fence. We were just inside the area we were supposed to stay in. If we had made it around the bottom of the cliff we would have been in big trouble. Lieutenant B. pulled out his cell phone and made a call, and soon a white van arrived to take us back to the "comforts" of our ship.

While we waited for the van, Lieutenant B. instructed us that this story was never to leave that spot. All of the aspects of safety and responsibility had been disregarded and thrown out the window, and he didn't want to have to answer for them. Not to mention the fact that he had clearly been scared to death.

Lieutenant B. also said I was the only one with whom he would ever discuss what had just happened, because I had achieved it without help. He also admitted the only reason he had started up the crevice was because he didn't intend to let some girl do something that he didn't or couldn't.

Well, this girl did it. Although scared and unsure, she did it.

Afterward, while on the ship and going about our normal duties and watch schedules, every time I ran into Lieutenant B. I would ask, "Read any good cliffhangers lately?"

He would just chuckle and nod.

India Roderick
U.S. Coast Guard

# THIRTY-EIGHT

*"For a people who are free, and who mean to remain so,*
*a well-organized and armed militia is their best security."*
Thomas Jefferson

Sergeant First Class Sharon Roberts joined the Women's Army Corps in 1975. She was stationed in Hawaii as a newlywed, and worked as an instructor at Utah's Military Academy for nine years. She rates her twenty years of service right up there with motherhood, and claims she couldn't have done it without the support of her family.

## I COULDN'T HAVE DONE IT WITHOUT YOU

While stationed at Fort Campbell, Kentucky, as a truck driver with the 102$^{nd}$ Transportation Company, I hauled fuel for the 101st Airborne Division, and handled "hot fueling" for their helicopters.

In 1976 I went to Germany for REFORGER (Return of Forces to Germany), a strategic military exercise, or war games during the Cold War, involving the United States and other members of the North Atlantic Treaty.

Although we expected to be housed in barracks the first few days and then go on to Tent City, we set up pup tents our first night, and got showers in a tent with cold water. But I figured things would get better once we picked up our trucks and got down to business.

And it did – we went to the field in the Black Forest, with our main location being in Tent City. Because there were only eighteen females among the more than 10,000 soldiers present at this exercise, we had a large tent surrounded by concertina wire. But the men were always using our shower.

I didn't get to go back to Tent City for the three weeks I spent in the field, so my assistant driver and I had to figure out a way to shower and get our uniforms clean. Let me tell you, the Rhine River is really cold in September. And just try to find feminine products when you don't speak the language. Despite all my gestures and attempts to explain, no one knew what I was talking about. Never had I been so embarrassed in my life.

Almost every day I went into the railhead to fill my tanker so I could perform my mission – fueling helicopters in the woods. I looked forward to these trips because I had met a very nice old couple in the town of Dinklesbule.

The first time I met the gentleman we were both buying cookies at a sweet shop, and he wanted to trade a German cigarette for one of my Kools. Well, that was out of the question since I had already tried that brand of cigarette and had nearly choked on the very strong flavor. But I had a half pack of smokes with me so I went ahead and gave him those.

After that he brought his wife with him every day, and we would sit and have a Coke and a bratwurst on a hard roll, at a little stand like the ones in Central Park. During these visits I learned a lot about the countryside, and they got to practice their English.

They even told me how they had fed and sheltered American soldiers in WWII. Although they had had little food for themselves and the winters were very hard, they tried to keep the soldiers warm and fed until they could get them out of the country and into France.

They told me how they had helped an American pilot escape from the Nazis after his plane went down in the Black Forest, and how he had in turn taught them to speak English.

Once, when ten Americans had been separated from their company, this couple hid them for three days in their bedroom, the attic, and in the shed outside their house because they didn't think the Germans would suspect them of hiding the enemy inside their very home.

Although the Germans searched their barn, and stayed nearby for several days, they never did search the house. Despite living in fear of being caught and shot on sight as traitors, this couple said they would do it all again.

Often, these Americans gave them personal trinkets as thanks for their help.

One young man had even given them an engagement ring that had been returned to him in a Dear John letter, so the German soldiers wouldn't get it if he were captured.

Although I was only in Dinklesbule for a short time it remains one of the most memorable weeks of my career. Because of this couple, I carried a little bit of history with me when I left.

Though I wanted to go to Panama when it came time to re-up, things were too unstable there and women weren't allowed to go into those areas – quite a change from today's Army. So I went to Hawaii. Married and Hawaii, what a honeymoon!

Several years later, after my discharge from active duty, I returned to the mainland and joined the Army National Guard, where I continued my military career for twenty years.

Without the support of my family, I would have failed as a soldier and missed out on so many wonderful experiences and opportunities. Thank you Blain, Kristopher, Terra and Tracy. I couldn't have done it without you!

Sergeant First Class Sharon Roberts, (retired)
Army National Guard

# THIRTY-NINE

*"On becoming soldiers, we have not ceased to be citizens."*
Oliver Cromwell

In 1977, Colonel Linda P. Higgins enlisted in the Army National Guard. She was the first female in the state of Utah to become a non-medical commissioned officer, and to wear a maternity uniform. In her twenty-eight years of service, she has held six commands, and enjoyed a career filled with memorable people and experiences.

## FROM THE HOT SEAT TO THE ALTAR

Fresh out of jump school, I found myself feeling a little depressed. It had been a tough experience, and I had had things said and done to me as one of the only two women to graduate that people would probably go to jail for today.

A lot of instructors there had never had a female student, and they hadn't been very excited about having us around. So there had been a lot of animosity, and we were either treated as a threat, or as babies. This was before the days of Equal Opportunity, before you couldn't say certain things and you had to be civil, or tolerant of each other.

So I was glad to be back in Utah, where I believed women were treated with respect.

While preparing to make my first or cherry jump with my new unit, I was in Camp Williams, and really nervous because it would be from a helicopter, and I had never done that.

As we waited for the aircraft to get loaded up, the jumpmaster, a friend of mine who had taken me under his wing, went over to brief the pilots. When he finished, he walked back to me snickering and shaking his head.

I asked him what the matter was, and he said, "Well, the pilot said he didn't want any dumb broads in his aircraft."

I had had it with this derogatory attitude and I intended to straighten these guys out. As I turned toward the helicopter, the jumpmaster said, "You can't go over there, those guys are officers."

I was only an E-4, but I didn't care. "I've had it," I said. "They can throw me out of the Army if they want, but I'm going to tell that guy what I think of his comment."

So I marched over to the helicopter and flung open the door, not realizing the pilot sits in the right seat, rather than the left.

When I opened the door this guy turned to look at me, and all I could see were black goggles and the name Higgins stamped on his helmet. But I laid into him and told him what I thought. And I just went on and on and on and then I pushed the door shut and walked over to my friend, who started laughing.

"Now what?" I asked.

"You just chewed out the wrong guy."

"You know what?" I said. "That guy's never going to see me again, so what do I care." Then I put on my chute and made my jump.

Some time later, when I had made second lieutenant and worked as assistant to the adjutant general's protocol officer, I became assigned to a committee to help the governor throw a huge party for the general who was about to retire.

When I learned I was expected to host the party in my uniform, and the governor anticipated me and my date to sit at the head table with him and his wife, I panicked.

I wasn't dating anyone at the time, and I had also found that back then men seemed to be threatened by military women. In fact, I didn't know any men that would be caught dead with a woman in uniform.

I started crying on a friend's shoulder about how I had to find a date for this big reception that would be seen with a woman wearing dress blues.

He said, "You know, I have a really good friend who's a pilot in the Guard. He'd go with you."

I brightened at the thought. "Do you really think he would?"

"Oh yeah," he said, "and he'd wear his uniform, too, so you won't feel too weird."

I agreed, and he set up a blind date.

When my doorbell rang on the night of the party, there stood this guy in dress blues. I immediately recognized the name on his uniform and realized he was the pilot I had chewed out. I felt really embarrassed.

I asked him if he remembered me, and when he said yes, I told him I applauded his bravery for showing up.

He just laughed, and said he'd looked forward to meeting me. "I've never had a woman talk to me like that. I guess I was curious."

As it turned out he didn't mind being seen with a woman in uniform, and we've been together now for twenty-four years.

Colonel Linda P. Higgins
Army National Guard

# FORTY

*"Do your damnedest in an ostentatious manner all the time."*
General George Patton, Jr.

In 1975, Michele Hunter Mirabile joined the Women's Army Corps. Shortly after her discharge in 1977 she signed up with the Utah Army National Guard, where she met and married her husband of twenty-five years. She loves to read, write, and travel with her family.

## EMERGENCY ESSENTIALS

Add a little stress, fatigue, a diet of C-rations, and *voila,* all systems are off – especially for a woman, and that unmentionable time of month.

When my cycle started early one summer while training with the 396th Aviation Company, I was three days into a two-week camp in the desert, desperate, and in need of a confidant.

Forced to swallow my pride, I approached my co-worker, and between the two of us we decided the best way to handle the situation was to make a dash to a nearby medical station occupied by the Air Force, in hopes they'd have appropriate sanitary supplies.

My commander was off flying a mission, and I had his Jeep. With rocks pinging against our undercarriage, we bounded over the uneven terrain, dodging potholes and stirring up enough dust to give our location away for miles in the distance.

At the small outstation, a technician promptly produced a bag of antiquated pads. Though he appeared happy to help, he seemed even more delighted to get them off his shelf.

I accepted his offering with trepidation. The bag looked like it had been left over from WWII, and the seemingly abnormal length and width of the pads led me to determine that not only had they been designed by a man, but by NASA.

But desperation makes one humble. So with pads in hand, I headed back to camp, hoping my commander hadn't showed up needing his vehicle.

But he was there, impatient and understandably perturbed – until he caught sight of the huge, bulging pads. For an instant he was powerless, the tables had been turned. He knew how to prepare his men for battle, but he was unprepared for my dilemma.

He swallowed hard, overlooked the shortcomings of a naïve young woman, and did what he could to soften the trauma of an already embarrassing moment.

Mustering his authority, he sent me back to the city in a helicopter leaving to collect parts, with orders to meet the pilot at the hangar first thing in the morning prepared for future female emergencies, and ready to resume my duties as a soldier.

Michele Hunter Mirabile
Army National Guard

# FORTY-ONE

*"War is the remedy that our enemies have chosen,*
*and I say let us give them all they want."*
General William T. Sherman

Major Liesl R. Carter began flying lessons at the age of sixteen. In 1993 she graduated from the Air Force Academy, and has been flying the KC-135 Stratotanker for the past ten years. Her supportive husband is a stay-at-home day for their young son, Maxwell.

## ON A WING AND A PRAYER

Even as a child, I had a fascination with flight and the space program, and so my parents gave me flying lessons at the age of sixteen to either cure me of my desire to fly, or to see if I really liked it. It turned out to be the latter, and I took lessons on and off throughout high school.

Then I started to wonder how I could get paid for flying.

My dad had been in the military, and I found myself drawn in that direction. And since the Air Force provided the best opportunities for females to fly, I applied to the Air Force Academy.

Upon graduation in 1993, I went to Vance AFB, Oklahoma, for Undergraduate Pilot Training, where I flew T-37s and T-38s. The T-37 is kind of a pig, meaning the engines are not very responsive, and it is hot in the summer and cold in the winter. The T-38, however, is sleek and fast, kind of like a mini fighter jet.

In March 1995, I was assigned to fly the KC-135 Stratotankers at Fairchild AFB, Washington. This plane is very versatile, and its missions range from aerial refueling to combat refueling in a hostile area, and from cargo delivery missions to aero-medical evacuations. They are also used to carry units into austere places such as Africa, as well as to interact with the public at air shows.

The KC-135 is also a great plane to fly. It is a stick-and-rudder aircraft, meaning none of the controls are hydraulically actuated. I like the fact that this aircraft seems to talk to me. I've been flying it for nearly ten years now, and I've become attuned to the correct feel and sound for various phases of flight.

As an aircraft commander, I sit in the left seat and would be known in the civilian world as captain. I am responsible for making sure the aircraft, the crew, and anyone else on board stays safe. Being in command of an aircraft that can reach speeds of up to 400 miles per hour is humbling, and I take my job very seriously.

One of my most vivid memories began on an exceptionally cold day in February 1999, during the Bosnia Campaign, when my scheduler called to say, "Hey, we need to pull you for TDY. We're sending you to Spain for ten days . . . tops."

Temporary duty isn't uncommon, so I didn't think much about it as I packed up my gear and headed out for what turned out to be a five-and-a-half month trip!

From Spain, I went to Italy. And in March, when Operation Allied Force kicked off, my crew flew missions mainly out into the

Macedonia region, refueling all kinds of aircraft to include fighters, both U.S. and NATO; sometimes KC-10s, which are a larger type of tanker or refueling aircraft; and AWACs, an airborne command and control aircraft.

One of the first nights of the war, while sitting alert with my crew, we got a call to launch. So the four of us rushed out to the jet, and seventeen minutes later we were off the ground and flying away. An F-117 had been shot down near Belgrade, and our gas was needed in this area as fast as we could get it there.

Belgrade, however, was one of the most heavily defended areas, and not all of the surface-to-air missile sites, or anti-aircraft defenses, had yet been taken out.

When we got to the specified location, the E-3 AWACs informed us of our mission, which involved refueling a KC-10 and dragging it toward the combat search-and-rescue area so it could refuel the airborne CSAR assets at the scene.

While I flew the aircraft, the boom operator worked in the back refueling the KC-10, and my co-pilot monitored the radios that were just crazy, in an effort to listen up and stay informed of the ongoing situation.

I had been in combat before. And thank goodness my navigator had been in combat. But my co-pilot and my boom operator had never been in an operational area.

My navigator plotted our course, keeping track of missile threat rings and giving me vectors toward our assigned area. He had the big picture of where we were, where we were going, and what areas to avoid so we wouldn't get shot down.

I looked at him over my right shoulder and said, "Jason, whatever you do, just keep us safe."

While flying at 350 miles per hour and skirting missile rings, we refueled the KC-10, and dragged it into the combat search-and-rescue area.

We turned off most of our aircraft lighting to give us more stealth, and to make us less of a target in case anyone from the ground decided to take a shot at us. And all the while my adrenaline rushed higher than ever before.

When we had off-loaded pretty much all our fuel, we scooted out of there on what we call bingo fuel, which is just enough gas to get back to your field.

Because of our efforts, rescue personnel retrieved that F-117 pilot. And that mission remains one of the most satisfying I've every flown.

Major Liesl R. Carter
U.S. Air Force

# FORTY-TWO

*"I have nothing to offer but blood, toil, tears, and sweat."*
Sir Winston Churchill

Lieutenant Commander Doreen L. Baldwin loves dogs and camping. She joined the Navy in 1980, lured by the promise of equal pay for equal work. In addition, the Iran Hostage Crisis was ongoing, and she wanted to be a part of the resolution. As a member of the Navy Reserve, she heads the department of Communications and Information Systems.

## IN THE SERVICE OF MY COUNTRY

Of all the things I could have found at a yard sale, I found Dickens, an eight-week-old Yellow Lab, who had just arrived at his foster family's home.

It's amazing how external events can have such a profound effect on us, and can even alter the direction of our lives. We all remember Hurricane Katrina, and where we were when the space shuttle crashed and the towers fell, and how these circumstances impacted us. And I will never forget this *PAWS With a Cause* puppy, who changed my life in immeasurable ways.

*PAWS With A Cause* is an organization that trains dogs to help the disabled live more productive lives. These dogs become amazing animals that can open doors, help clients in and out of wheelchairs, pick up dropped items, give money to cashiers, bring clients the phone and even do basic laundry.

I had heard of *PAWS* and was aware some local families raised puppies for them, and by the time my family was ready to leave that day in August 2001, I had Dickens' business card, a basic understanding of the foster puppy program, and a desire to learn more.

I also had a nagging question: How would I be able to raise a dog for a year and then give it away?

My own dogs, a pair of Golden Retrievers, had been my constant companions until earlier that year when I had lost twelve-year-old Rusty to cancer. It had been devastating, and I still missed him deeply. Shamrock, at age thirteen, still thought she was a pup, but her body told us otherwise and I knew it would only be a matter of time before I'd be saying goodbye to her as well.

I had had a full life with these dogs, and endless memories to help me through their loss. So how could I let my heart get attached to another cuddly bundle of fur and then give it up?

I had always been drawn to service-oriented occupations, however, and consider it a privilege to provide others with what they need to accomplish great things. In fact, the common theme in all I do seems to revolve around the service of others.

Prior to entering the military I worked in information technology, writing code and providing troubleshooting support. On active duty, I was an electronic technician who fixed equipment used for communication, providing a service to those who used it. As a teacher, I served my students, guiding them as they learned about computer networking. And even now, as a Navy officer trained through hard work and discipline to serve my country, I certify future command structures for NATO, and serve my troops by removing obstacles and fostering their growth and performance.

With *PAWS*, I could serve my community, while providing a service to those with physical disabilities by training future assistance dogs. And as I thought about the countless ways these dogs allowed someone with disabilities to live the life you and I take for granted, I decided to get involved.

The first step following the application consisted of a home visit. When I heard "home visit" it translated "inspection." I'm sure that's held over from my active duty days but I knew I would be on display. Therefore, the day of the visit my house was immaculate, and my dog groomed and on her best behavior.

After countless questions and detailed explanations of the requirements for puppy raisers, I got a chance to make my request. The *PAWS* liaison explained to me that I could request the puppy's sex, breed, or both. But the more specific I was, the longer I might have to wait.

Because I knew I wanted a female, and the two breeds prevalent in the *PAWS* breeding program were Labs and Golden Retrievers, I devised a plan I felt sure to be foolproof, that also answered the nagging question of how I could part with the dog after a year. I loved Golden Retrievers, their personalities and their temperaments. So I'd choose a Lab.

And so began the wait. I waited, and waited and waited until I couldn't wait any more. The home visit had been in early April. By May I'd heard nothing and the anticipation proved too much. I called *PAWS* hoping for some news and got the best. I'd be getting my puppy in early July – a female Black Lab from the "O" litter.

My first assignment was to submit three names to be considered by the board. Excited to have a say in her name, I chose Onyx, Oakley, Oreo and Ono in that order.

On July 2, 2002 I signed the paperwork for and brought home the most precious, eight-week-old little girl named Onyx. She came complete with collar, leash, crate, initial food supply and the most adorable "Future Assistance Dog" cape.

My mission was to train her in the basics and introduce her to as many experiences as possible. She needed to go to stores, ride in elevators and public transportation, and meet people from all walks of life. For the next ten to twelve months I would be responsible for all expenses associated with the completion of this mission. *PAWS* would supply free vet services and obedience classes, and everything else would be tax deductible.

Shamrock took to Onyx right away. Having a puppy in the house brought some of the puppy back out in her and she acted five years younger.

Fourth of July at my house is synonymous with camping and the outdoors, and this year would be no different. Shamrock, Onyx and I loaded up the camper and were off to meet up with family and friends for the long weekend. Onyx would soon come to know this was a family of dog lovers, and her new friends would help ease the pain of separation from her mom and siblings.

Those first few weeks I took Onyx everywhere from Mackinaw Island to shopping at the mall and the local grocery store. She learned fast and did amazingly well. It had been twelve years since I'd had a puppy and I'd almost forgotten how much went into the first few weeks. But she made it seem easy.

Week two *PAWS* had a picnic for all puppy raisers. It would be our first official outing with them, and I was excited and nervous at the same time. As fate would have it, I parked next to someone who looked very familiar; it was Natalie, the raiser of Dickens. How appropriate that the person who started me on this journey was there to welcome me to this event. Even more ironic was the fact that she now raised Oakleigh, Onyx's sister.

Nervousness quickly gave way to belonging. The *PAWS* raisers turned out to be a group of dog lovers all working toward a common goal. Many of them had raised multiple dogs and freely gave advice and encouragement. It was truly a family.

Week three began Onyx's first obedience class at *PAWS*. But they were very specific about not bringing sick puppies to class, and since Onyx had been acting a little lethargic, I called ahead to make sure it'd be okay to come. We determined the lethargy was probably due to her teething, and since she needed shots and would be seeing the vet anyway, I received the green light.

As it turned out, Onyx had a fever and was clearly not just teething. We were thoroughly reprimanded and sent home with meds and a treatment plan. Although the *PAWS* vet was a free service, I found myself wondering if the price had been worth the bedside manner.

Onyx's condition worsened. The lethargy grew into an inability to use the left side of her body. Remembering our treatment at our last visit to the vet, I opted to take her to my own dog's vet.

For the past two weeks I'd stood vigil over this sick pup and we'd bonded beyond words. But six hundred dollars in vet bills and two hospital stays later she still had not improved.

I called Julie, the Foster Puppy Program Coordinator, and arranged to bring Onyx in for observation. Since the *PAWS* staff vet was on vacation, she made an appointment with one of their local contracted veterinarians and invited me along.

The vet quickly determined that Onyx had strangles, a disease normally found in horses and similar to chicken pox in people. While it usually showed up as external pustules, it could also attack the joints, which was Onyx's case. Thankfully the vet was able to prescribe medication, and Julie allowed me to take Onyx home.

Through it all I learned that although *PAWS* is a caring and compassionate organization, sometimes a dog had to be released for the sake of the business. Fortunately, this had not been one of those times.

Onyx improved daily, and was soon her old self. We were back on track, and it was time to restart her training. But she wouldn't be fully immunized until six months of age, so her first official puppy class had to wait until October.

Due to my first attempt at an obedience class, I was a little nervous to try it again. So I opted for the afternoon class where there would be less people. Imagine my surprise when all the dogs began showing up in costume!

Apparently puppy raisers take Halloween very seriously. So that afternoon, Onyx and I went to Wal-Mart and settled on pirate costumes – a hat, cape and earring for Onyx, and a hat and eye patch for me – and went to the night class.

But as it turned out, night standards were a few notches higher. Although we didn't win any prizes, we had experienced the side of *PAWS* we'd been missing – the interaction with other raisers and dogs, especially in a non-threatening and fun environment.

Onyx flourished in the next few months and moved quickly through the levels within obedience class. She passed her AKC

Canine Good Citizen test and received her certificate. But she had issues with stairs. If they weren't carpeted, she wouldn't use them.

Although I had been working on this for months and her improvement varied with the day, two months before her scheduled formal training, I noticed yet another phobia – slippery or shiny surfaces frightened her. Even the floor of the training facility was now a source of anxiety. Overcoming these two issues would play a big part in whether or not she'd make it as an assistance dog.

When a dog is ready to come in for formal training, what is referred to as simply "the letter" is sent to the raiser, containing the final questionnaire which when filled out and returned, begins the call-in process. Although procrastination can extend this process for a short time, in the long run separation is inevitable.

Twelve months ago my plan to get a Lab because it would be easier to turn in than a Golden, had sounded really good. But all Onyx and I had been through had changed everything. Additionally, I had been told that overlapping dogs helps a little. I had listened to this advice and was currently raising my second dog, ASAP.

But the bottom line is nothing takes away the pain of letting go. I arranged things so Onyx would be turned in just prior to me catching a plane for Las Vegas, hoping the trip would take my mind off missing her.

As Onyx and I sat on the tailgate of my Yukon saying goodbye, I gave her one last piece of advice. I said, "If you want to come home, just don't do the stairs." If a dog doesn't make it in formal training, the puppy raiser gets the option of taking it back into their home as a pet. While I wanted her to succeed, I knew I'd take her back without hesitation.

I had been in Vegas for three days when I received the call. Onyx never had time to fail the stairs because she couldn't get past the slippery floors of the kennel. Julie told me all dogs get at least a week in the kennel before they are career changed, but for Onyx, they made an exception.

Repeat raisers say the dog chooses its career, and I believe Onyx chose me. She knew I'd need her to get through losing Shamrock, and to assist me as I continued to raise foster puppies.

Together we have gone on to raise five additional puppies. ASAP, a beautiful Golden Retriever who from the time she was a puppy carried herself with pride and purpose, is now certified as a seizure response dog in the state of Washington.

Rizzo, my feistiest Golden Retriever named after the character in Grease, lived up to her name and had an inner spark that attracted everyone. She chose not to certify despite her ability to do so, because she knew an eight-year-old boy needed her more. This boy is too young to have a certified dog, so as a social support dog Rizzo can use the tasks she learned to provide him freedom. More importantly she has provided that special bond between a boy and his dog.

Quattro, a Yellow Lab, was the first dog I received halfway through the training process. Her initial raiser was no longer able to care for her so she needed a new home. Quattro was born to be a service dog. She was by far the easiest dog for me and all the formal trainers at *PAWS* as well. She is currently in the process of certifying with her client as a wheelchair assistance dog.

Kona, a Chocolate Lab, was donated to the program by the Foster Puppy Coordinator, who personally asked me to raise her. While you bond to all these dogs in different ways, this one has definitely carved a special place in my heart. Along with puppy raisers, *PAWS* has foster families who care for the breeding stock.

As I've agreed to do this with Kona, it looks as though Onyx and I will soon have another addition to our family.

Lastly, is Shasta, a Lab/Golden mix, the second dog I've received halfway through the training process. She is my challenge. It's true that it's much easier to teach good habits than to undo bad ones. We struggle daily, but she continues to make progress and will soon choose her destiny.

Through the years of raising and turning in future assistance dogs, I have come to realize there is no easy answer to the question, "How can you give them back?" Nevertheless, it is a wonderful feeling to help someone gain his or her independence, and the experience has forever changed my life.

Lieutenant Commander Doreen L. Baldwin
U.S. Navy Reserve

# FORTY-THREE

*"Never tell people how to do things.*
*Tell them what to do and they will surprise you with their ingenuity."*
General George Patton, Jr.

In 1977, Colonel Linda P. Higgins enlisted in the Army National Guard. She was the first female in the state of Utah to become a non-medical commissioned officer, and to wear a maternity uniform. In her twenty-eight years of service, she has held six commands, and enjoyed a career filled with memorable people and experiences.

## SURVIVAL OF THE FITTEST

When I signed up with the 19th Special Forces in 1977, I was a more energetic and less intelligent woman than I am today. But I wanted to jump, so I worked hard to get physically fit and headed off to jump school.

Prior to that time, Fort Benning, Georgia, was the official U.S. Army Jump School. But the expense of transporting soldiers from the Western United States to Georgia had become expensive and time-consuming, so command channels of the Special Forces had come up with an alternative plan to conduct training at the U.S. Forest Service Smokejumper School in Missoula, Montana.

I was in that first experimental class.

While the school had all the necessary equipment and facilities, the 19th SF Group provided the support staff, and Fort Benning provided a team of Airborne instructors known as Tacs, or "Black Hats." Named after their distinctive hats that define them as staff, these instructors are physically fit screaming machines who can out run, out jump, and out yell the average soldier.

When I got off the bus one of them said, "I didn't know women would be part of this training." Another one even asked me why I wasn't home barefoot and pregnant.

Fortunately the Army has come a long way since that time, when women were a novice in the National Guard, let alone Special Forces.

In my class, seven females began training, but by the third day only two remained. In fact, we started out with a total of 115 soldiers. But after injuries, quitters, and dismissals, only forty-seven made it to graduation.

Our first day, we were introduced to a term we came to dread – suspended agony. This portion of training consisted of a series of approximately twenty parachute harnesses suspended from scaffolding, elevated about six feet off the ground and surrounded by a thin boardwalk. The object was to place yourself in the harness, step off the boardwalk and hang there for up to an hour while the Tacs drilled you on emergency procedures and graded your immediate response.

Another piece of equipment used in training was a section of an airplane fuselage with a rear door, known as the tower. We would put on a harness, and on command run up the four flights of stairs

192

that zigzagged to the fuselage. Each time our right foot hit a stair we would yell, "I want to be Airborne!"

Once inside the fuselage, which was approximately forty feet off the ground, we were connected to a system of cables and pulleys attached to telephone poles, and on command we would simulate jumping from the aircraft while performing our best-tucked jump position.

The cables then ran at a slight angle to the ground, where a fellow student would catch us just prior to slamming into the mattress at the end of the slant.

In addition to these training exercises that caused us a great deal of discomfort and chafing, every morning before breakfast we would run several miles up and down the runways, carrying a rucksack that weighed a minimum of sixty pounds. Needless to say, most of us had very sore inner thighs on a daily basis.

In an effort to ease our suffering, my bunkmate Barbara and I hatched an idea.

Because females had never trained at this site before, the small post exchange that had been set up in the basement of one of the barracks had only been stocked with toiletries and clothing for men. So when Barbara and I made a request for feminine hygiene products, the command sent a captain out to take our order just prior to his making a run into town for supplies.

We requested and paid for an entire case of Kotex, ignoring the look of surprise on that poor captain's face. No doubt he wondered why only two women needed so many pads for a three-week course.

When he returned with our purchase we promptly began the task of selling the extra-thick sanitary pads, at our cost, to our fellow students for protection of their inner thighs, along with medical tape to secure them.

The next morning, as Barbara and I ran at the front of the formation where we were often placed because our stride was shorter than the average male's, we turned around at the halfway point to return to start, and saw a mile-long trail of pads down the runway.

The Tacs halted formation and began scratching their heads. For one rare moment they were speechless.

While they decided how to address the situation, they issued push-ups as punishment for littering the runway, and it was all we could do not to laugh.

Because we ran in our jump boots, we didn't have to blouse, or tuck in the hem of our trousers, and the pads had dropped out of pant legs. Obviously the men hadn't developed a reliable technique of securing their Kotex.

Colonel Linda P. Higgins
Army National Guard

# FORTY-FOUR

*"Take calculated risks."*
General George Patton, Jr.

Chief Master Sergeant Kenna White has been a member of the Air National Guard since 1974. When she isn't solving administration problems for airmen and soldiers, she enjoys quilting, golfing, and camping with her family.

## A REWARDING PLACE TO HANG YOUR HAT

Thirty years ago, while attending college, I accepted a temporary hire technician job as an administrative assistant with a unit in the Utah Air National Guard. I thought a ninety-day position would pay me enough to cover my tuition for the next term.

I was not a member of the Guard, nor had I ever considered joining. But when my temporary job ended, my unit offered me a full-time technician position contingent on the fact I would have to join the Air National Guard. I was very shy, and terrified at the thought of going to basic training. But I decided to go for it.

All the way home, I thought of my mother and my boyfriend, and wondered how I would tell them of my decision. Although they were surprised, they were very supportive.

I had never been in an airplane before, and the day I headed off for basic I was extremely nervous. And by the time I had reached San Antonio, Texas, I wanted to turn back. To make matters worse, the moment I got on the bus heading for Lackland Air Force Base the instructors started yelling. Over the course of the next few weeks the yelling never stopped. I heard it from the minute I woke up until the moment I went to bed.

That first week of boot camp was the worst time of my life. For a sheltered girl, being thrown into the hostile environment of boot camp was jarring and had me wondering what in the world I had gotten myself into.

After a week of grueling harassment we were finally able to call home, and the minute I heard my boyfriend's voice I started sobbing, and telling him I didn't know why I had ever signed up. It was so good to hear a kind, sympathetic voice.

Now, I am a chief master sergeant. As a matter of fact, I became the first female chief in the Utah Air National Guard. Over the years I have worked as an administrative specialist, supply technician, and first sergeant. Currently I work in the Human Resources Office for both the Utah Air and Army National Guard full-time technician force. I have also traveled to several countries, and almost every state in the union.

When I joined the Guard, there were only five women on the Air Guard base. Now there are hundreds. And all of them are sharp, dedicated and proud of their country.

The military is a wonderful and rewarding place to hang your hat, and I'm so glad I went for it thirty years ago.

Chief Master Sergeant Kenna White
Air National Guard

# FORTY-FIVE

*"A battery of field artillery is worth a thousand muskets."*
General William T. Sherman

In 1980, Colonel Margaret M. Cameron was commissioned as a second lieutenant in the Army Nurse Corps. Currently, she is serving a tour as Case Management Supervisor for the Community Based Health Care Organization. She enjoys dancing and tennis, and highly recommends the military experience to any male or female.

## THE THINGS WE HOLD MOST DEAR

Because of my mother's example and her experiences as a nurse, I went to college and became an RN, where I learned very young that many individuals with health problems had made numerous unhealthy choices over the years.

As a result, my goal became learning about the body, educating others, and understanding the dynamics of human behavior in order to impact others to be advocates of their own health care.

When I moved away from the comfort of friends and family in Chicago, to the sunny days in Arizona, I met and began dating a handsome helicopter pilot in the National Guard, and started accompanying him to military functions.

I thoroughly enjoyed the camaraderie of all the talented professionals serving their country I came in contact with. Due to my own appreciation and love for this country that had been enhanced by a summer of traveling through Europe, when he encouraged me to volunteer with the National Guard, I signed up, and was commissioned as a second lieutenant in March 1980.

I became the only female in an artillery unit in Mesa, Arizona, and was assigned as the field nurse to support the battalion on firing missions. Not being one to hurry up and wait, or twiddle my thumbs, I started teaching the soldiers first aid, CPR and health education.

I admit that more partying went on in the field in those days, and on more than one occasion I chewed a little Red Man tobacco to fit in. Fortunately we have a much healthier military now that adheres to zero tolerance for drinking, discourages smoking, encourages physical fitness, weight maintenance and equality in opportunity.

Presently, I have the privilege of being the Deputy Commander of the Medical Command, Utah National Guard. In support of Operation Enduring Freedom, I have been asked to complete a tour as the Case Management Supervisor for the CBHC (Community Based Health Care Organization).

The Reserve and Guard have special challenges because, unlike regular Army, many of the soldiers are based in sites that don't have quick access to hospitals at major military installations.

Three years ago, the Utah Guard ran a pilot program incorporating many of the concepts of disability management. When the Army decided to improve its services to wounded Reserve and Guard soldiers, it developed a program based largely on the Utah model. Since then, the Army has hired or mobilized 780 physicians, nurses, clerks and case managers to serve these soldiers, called "medical holdovers."

This is a voluntary program for part-time soldiers to remain on active duty while they are recovering or going through medical administrative board procedures as they work within their limitations, in jobs that range from working at National Guard armories to helping with rear detachments of mobilized units.

Because of this far-sighted program, based on the belief that an individual will recover quicker at their home with support of family and friends, hundreds of medical holdovers now receive treatment in their hometowns on a daily basis. Their disabilities range from illness, IED injuries, mental health issues and re-integration challenges, to loss of a part of self, identity, job or family.

Though I've have had my own difficult times of challenge over the past twenty-six years of service, I've grown as a woman. And yes, I've often had to work harder, expend more effort, balance more priorities, and keep my nose cleaner than my male counterparts in the system, but for females, that seems to be the standard.

As a single mother, I have commuted over the past twenty years from San Diego to Salt Lake City to attend monthly drills, and my son, who has borne the brunt of sacrifice, has supported me with little complaint. He is my hero.

My experience as an officer in the Army Nurse Corps has given me perspective, direction, and a connection to what I consider the most dedicated selfless patriots who believe in this great country.

As an American citizen, it is heartening to know that the things we hold most dear are what our military stands for and defends on a daily basis. I highly recommend the military experience to any male or female in order to make their lives richer.

Colonel Margaret M. Cameron
Army National Guard

# FORTY-SIX

*"There is no victory at bargain basement prices."*
General Dwight D. Eisenhower

Marine Science Technician Tosha M. Crow has served in the Coast Guard since 2003. She assists in facility and vessel inspections, investigates oil spills and vessel mishaps, and is involved with port state control. She is a big fan of fine arts, and enjoys computer and video gaming.

## LONG DISTANCE LOVE

Already in a failing marriage, the last thing I wanted when I joined the Coast Guard and went to A-school was another relationship. Though I did meet a lot of great people I still keep in touch with, I expected little more from the experience than a career and some rank.

On my first day at the Yorktown training site, Kira, a girl I had just met in class, and I were walking when she caught sight of AJ, an old friend she had lost track of. They hugged, relived old times, and didn't seem able to catch up fast enough. I listened for a moment and then excused myself, since I didn't really know either of them.

Kira and I became friends over the eight-week course, and I talked with AJ a few times. Although I thought he was cool, not once did I think of him as anything other than another friend from Yorktown, so when I graduated and moved on to my next unit, I seldom gave him another thought.

Then my marriage finished falling apart.

While keeping in touch with Kira, mostly through e-mail, she suggested I write to AJ. Of course I did, and soon began talking to him on a regular basis. AJ is not an easy person to forget, no matter what your opinion of him. He is full of energy, his own person, and the life-of-the-party type. We found plenty to talk about.

As a joke in one e-mail, I said, "Why don't you come live up here where I'm stationed?"

When he asked why, I said, "Because I am here, why else?"

Apparently he hadn't heard that egotistical reply before and found it pretty amusing. He said he would visit, though, since the Christmas and New Year holidays were coming up and he didn't have other plans. I didn't have other plans either, and spending New Year's with a visitor instead of alone seemed like a great idea.

I picked him up at the airport, expecting an interesting holiday but nothing more. By now, I had been separated from my spouse for a while and had flirted around some, but I wasn't trying to start anything serious.

Afterward we kept in touch, but it didn't take long for us to realize AJ's short visit had sparked an interest in us both. AJ came out with it first, however, since I still shielded my emotions.

A month later, I visited him at his place. That visit went just as well as the first and the little spark grew. Soon our visits became a regular thing – between his underway schedules – and the little spark grew into a flame. Even though we didn't get to see much of each other, we got closer.

Within time, our crush turned into love. Now, a year later, we are still going uphill. Although we feel stronger about each other every time we are together, we are in the military and can't just pick up and leave when we want, or move nearer to each other.

Though it is great having someone in my life I feel so connected to, the relationship doesn't come without serious sacrifices. Even though we have been together for slightly more than a year, we have only spent a little over two month's actual time with each other. Our visits only last for a week or two, and since we live several states away and one of us has to travel either by plane or car, it's expensive.

Although we phone, e-mail, chat online, and do whatever we can to keep busy when we are apart, we can't call up and ask each other to come over for a hug when we're feeling lonely. And seeing each other's name on the other end of an Internet connection only reminds us of how much we miss being with them.

Most likely it will be another year before either of us has the opportunity to move closer. Maybe it will happen when I change my rate and go to school. But even then there are no guarantees, as the military sends you wherever they need you.

Although not seeing each other on a regular basis is difficult, we will keep meeting as often as we can manage, and hoping life works out to our advantage.

In the meantime, I will see AJ again in a month and a half. I will drive out to his place and we will go visit Kira. Then we will drive back to my place, and he'll fly home a week later. It will be a hectic vacation, but at least we'll be together.

We are looking forward to being stationed together in the future; it will definitely be a relief to us both. Eventually, the sacrifices we are making now will be worthwhile. After all, the harder one works for a prize, the more one relishes it in the end.

Petty Officer Tosha M. Crow
U.S. Coast Guard

# FORTY-SEVEN

*"We need to learn to set our course by the stars,*
*not by the lights of every passing ship."*
Omar Nelson Bradley

Debbie Kelner began her military career in 1978 as a Navy cook. Today, she is a member of the Army Reserve, and a veteran of Operation Enduring Freedom. She is grateful for the opportunities the military has given her to see the world and serve her country.

## AIN'T IT GREAT?

When I joined the Navy, I went to San Diego for basic training and A school.

I failed a phase in cooking school, however, and had to be set back two weeks, finishing up just as assignments were being issued.

They wanted to send me to Orlando, Florida, to cook for the recruits there at boot camp. But I didn't want to go. I wanted to get as far away as possible from anyplace that reminded me of any kind of training.

As it turned out, there was a gal – the number one student in our class – who was going to Adak, Alaska, and she didn't want to go there.

"Hey," I said, sensing an opportunity, "you can take my spot!"

Fortunately she liked the idea, so we traded. But as I packed up to go, one of my favorite chiefs said, "Kelner, I hear you're going to Adak."

"Yeah, ain't it great?"

"You're gonna hate it there," he said, "because you don't smoke, and you don't swear."

"I do . . . sometimes."

"Kelner, you're going to hate it there because you don't drink, and that's the only thing there is to do up there."

"I think I'm going to go anyway," I said.

So I headed off to Alaska, and do you know what I found? Adak is just a dot on the map, an island about thirty-five miles in diameter on the Aleutian Chain, where the weather changes every five minutes from bad to worse, and from worse to bad.

But I discovered I could do just about anything on that island I wanted. I even tried my hand at fishing. Everyday I'd see fly fishermen out at Thumb Bay, and everyday they used a different colored lure. They told me the pink ones were the best, so I got myself some gear and went fishing.

I never did catch anything, and once I threw my line out so far I hooked it on the other side of the river and had to cut it off. But what really ticked me off was this eagle that flew right down to the water and took off with the biggest fish I'd ever seen.

I also found myself a branch of my church. As it turned out, my captain was the president, so in essence he wore two hats. Every

Sunday when we flocked to his house he would say, "It's so nice that all my children can be here."

I really came to love these people. Life in the military can either make you or break you, and it can be especially difficult for a single woman. So I felt blessed and grateful to be surrounded by their support and influence.

America is the land of the brave and the free; a country made up of people with all kinds of beliefs from all corners of the world. It truly is the land of milk and honey.

Ain't it great?

Debbie Kelner
U.S. Navy

# FORTY-EIGHT

*"Part of the American dream is to live long and die young.*
*Only those Americans who are willing to die for their country are*
*fit to live."*
General Douglas MacArthur

In 1979, Captain Beverly G. Kelley became the first woman to command a Coast Guard cutter. At the end of a thirty-year career, she looks forward to tackling the full-time job of motherhood.

## YOU'VE COME A LONG WAY, BABY

In 1979, while operating out of Ketchikan, Alaska, I received orders to take command of a 95-foot Coast Guard patrol boat out of Maui. I stood duty at port call, feeling sick and miserable with a bad cold. But as soon as I opened up those papers, I ran out on the gangway, greeting all the sailors as they came on board and telling them I was going to Hawaii.

Junior officers are eligible to command a small cutter after completing their first tour of a large ship. So I had thrown my hat into the ring and had been waiting for the results of the selection board, where officers with the highest scores are either given command of a LORAN station or a cutter.

I had been given the *Cape Newagen*.

She was in a shipyard in Oahu, and I had to pick her up there. Because I reported on board a month before a woman in Florida, I became the first woman to command a cutter. As a result, I had to deal with the issues of the press, in addition to the challenge of learning my duties as commander, and I had no experience with either of these situations.

I caught on pretty quick, however, and learned to manage the press when I told one of the reporters who wanted to do follow up stories and reports of dramatic rescues that I would keep her informed if she promised not to make the entire story about me.

"I want you to mention other members of the crew in the article," I said, "so we all get equal time."

As a result, the crew got to enjoy some of the attention, and I would send those articles home to their mothers or grandmothers. This created great camaraderie, and they no longer minded the press coming on board.

For the most part, my crew had a terrific attitude. When one of our crewmembers – an electronic technician with a great sense of humor – was asked about having a female commander, he said, "Well, it's hardly any different than having a man on board, except when the wind blows over the bridge, the curtains knock over the flowerpots."

Once, the press asked if family was important to me and if I planned to start one anytime soon. I said, "Yes, someday."

But when the Sunday paper came out the article read, "Lieutenant Kelley wants to get married and have a baby right away."

I had said someday, and they had interpreted it to mean Sunday!

Another time, when interviewed by a Japanese paper, they altered my photos to slant my eyes.

My chief petty officer went out of his way to help the crew deal with having a female commander, and to help me deal with the press. It was a lot of work for him considering he was also the executive officer, or number two guy, which is a big job in itself.

When I came on board, he sat me down with a long list of topics for discussion.

We went over each item and talked about how things may or not be different. He expressed his support, and said he was kind of excited to be associated with the Coast Guard's new initiative regarding female leadership and really wanted it to work.

At one point when he got up to use the head, I grabbed his list and looked it over, and noticed one item on that list was "one-piece bathing suits."

I cracked up, and couldn't wait to see how he approached that topic. But when he came back and we resumed our discussion he never did bring it up.

At the end of my tour, I mentioned this to him and he was quite embarrassed. He said I'd seemed pretty mature so he'd just decided not to mention it.

Although I took that policy with me it's interesting to see how times changed, as years later a girl broached the topic with Human Relations, claiming women were being discriminated against by having to wear one-piece bathing suits.

After that, I just told my crew to use good taste – no Speedos or bikinis.

When I was a junior officer going through all my learning trials and tribulations including having to deal with the extra issues associated with being the first, I figured in twenty years it would be "no big deal" having women on cutters, and I was right.

Now, whenever I talk about the issues I had to deal with, young officers look at me with bewilderment. They can't understand why it was so strange and so difficult when women reported aboard. They remind me I am old. And that is great!

However, I find I carry baggage with me that servicewomen today do not, and I make a concerted effort to ensure that the USCG addresses issues that affect them in areas of health care, reproductive opportunities, and childcare. In my mind, the best way to describe the issues of the past is by referring to the words of the old cigarette ad, "You've come a long way, baby."

When it comes to shipboard and overall career opportunities for women in the U.S. Coast Guard, we have come a long way. Today, the Coast Guard does not restrict women in any way. All careers are open to them.

Now, the Service needs to address human resource issues like the above that affect today's women, and in most cases, men also.

I have had a great career. I love the Coast Guard and all we do as a Service, day in and day out. We make a difference in the United States and in the world.

In just a few short months I will happily tell people I am a Retired Coast Guardsman, and very proud of the opportunity I've had to serve my country.

Captain Beverly G. Kelley
U.S. Coast Guard

# FORTY-NINE

*"If you must break the law, do it to seize power:*
*in all other cases observe it."*
Julius Caesar

In 1975, Michele Hunter Mirabile joined the Women's Army Corps. Shortly after her discharge in 1977 she signed up with the Utah Army National Guard, where she met and married her husband of twenty-five years. She loves to read, write, and travel with her family.

## SNOWBUNNIES

In 1976, the Army still hadn't quite figured out what to do with women. As a result, the few of us stationed at Fort Richardson, Alaska, were housed in isolated barracks, near a wooded area on the far side of the installation, and had to cover a lengthy distance to get to and from our duty stations each day.

Although military police were said to patrol the area on a regular basis, in the land of the midnight sun, dangers lurking ranged from severe weather to encounters with wildlife in the form of moose and man, and were greatly enhanced by weeks of total darkness.

In addition, my first sergeant, a grizzled combat veteran fresh from the jungles of Vietnam, viewed women as a distraction and a burden. He seemed to go out of his way to keep his unit from being integrated, by assigning females duties elsewhere, and turning a blind eye to their needs and training.

Consequently, I escaped cold-weather indoctrination, which was pretty much considered mandatory for new arrivals at Fort Richardson. Along with basic survival skills, this exercise focused on learning how to survive in sub-zero temperatures by camping out in the snow, snowshoeing, cross-country skiing, rappelling, and crossing a frozen river.

When news of this "oversight" slipped out, my first sergeant decided to make some arctic training plans of his own, and about fifty other members of my unit and I were whisked away in Chinook helicopters, to a desolate expanse at the edge of a frozen lake.

Like my first sergeant, my commander and most of the other career soldiers I had met thus far in the military were wary of women, and weren't about to embrace thoughts of equality between the sexes, or incorporate the word "co-ed" into their vocabularies any time soon.

So, Linda, the only other female, and I were instructed to set up camp near the shore, and make ourselves comfortable until the helicopters returned for us in a day or two. The men would settle in about a hundred yards away, in a forested area on much higher ground.

When we reached our destination, we climbed out of the helicopter and stood shivering in the frosty air as we waited for the men to unload and hike to the top of the hill. As soon as the choppers were empty and heading for home, we began looking around for trees, rocks, or anything else we could anchor our shelter-halves to in order to provide relief from the onslaught of wind.

But the shore was barren, and as I removed my shelter-half from my backpack, it flapped hard in the gale then soared into the sky and far across the lake like a giant prehistoric bat.

Although we were equipped with warm sleeping bags and plenty of C-rations, the temperatures were well below zero, and the wind that tore at the fur-lined hoods of our parkas had blown away anything that even resembled kindling.

Linda sat huddled on the frozen ground, hugging her parka and looking at me with crystal-coated lashes and blue lips. "We're going to die," she said.

Too numb to argue, I hooked my thumb toward the hill where curls of smoke evidenced the success of our male counterparts, gathered my gear and headed for the incline. At this point an article fifteen had much more appeal than becoming a pillar of ice.

Women's fatigues were made of a much thinner fabric than men's. In addition, our boots were lightweight and smooth-soled, and our platoon sergeant had told us we wouldn't need our bunny boots as the exercise was short and the weather wasn't expected to be severe. Consequently, as we walked, our boots were about as effective as ice-skates, and the wind cut to our skin as though we were naked.

With each step I took as I crunched across the frozen terrain I sank to my knees through the icy crust. By the time we had made it about halfway up the hill I could no longer feel my toes.

As we neared the crest of the hill we were on our hands and knees, struggling against the slippery ground, and praying neither of us lost our grip and wound up having to make the trek a second time.

When we finally reached the top, we brushed the snow and ice from our uniforms hoping to look nonchalant and far less desperate than we felt, and trudged into the male campsite that now boasted a bon fire surrounded by soldiers heating their C-rations for dinner.

"Look," said one of the guys when he caught sight of us, "it's snowbunnies!"

With chattering teeth and icicle-draped noses, we nudged our way into the ring of bodies around the fire and stayed as close as possible to its warmth until the next day.

When we heard the whomp, whomp of the helicopters coming to take us back to civilization, we hustled down the hill and were standing on the frozen shore as our platoon sergeant stepped out of the aircraft.

He looked at our gear that sat packed and ready for loading, and nodded his head in approval. "See? It wasn't so bad now, was it?"

Linda and I just looked at each other and smiled. Nobody ever did mention the fact that our company had just had its first mixed-company training exercise, and that equality had *not* played a part.

Michele Hunter Mirabile
Women's Army Corps

# FIFTY

*" . . . but for a soldier his duty is plain. He is to obey the orders of all those placed over him and whip the enemy wherever he meets him."*
General Ulysses S. Grant

While in the Army, Leslie Watson served as a medic in Iraq and Korea. She is a student, athlete, and perfectionist, who credits her determination and stamina to wartime experiences.

## ICE-COLD SODAS

Shortly after Operation Iraqi Freedom, my lieutenant and I drove our Humvee into a nearby village one day to buy ice for the sodas he had purchased from a street vendor – heaven forbid he should go without those even in times of war.

Because we were Americans, all eyes were on us as we did a U-turn and parked behind an ice truck. The marketplace was really crowded, and I could feel panic growing inside me.

When a little boy came up to the driver's side door, my lieutenant starting bugging him about the ice and trying to get a cheaper price.

In the meantime, a crowd had amassed on the passenger's side of our vehicle. Although they were mostly kids who were just sort of staring at me, I couldn't help thinking that something was about to happen.

I had my M-16 on my lap where no one could see it, locked and loaded just in case. But I felt trapped, as we were stuck behind the ice truck and surrounded by a growing number of people.

By now, the first boy my lieutenant had been talking to was in the truck chopping ice, and my lieutenant was bartering with a different boy in an effort to get the ice even cheaper.

As I sat looking around, tasting panic and wishing we'd just get the heck out of there, something hit the window hard enough to shatter the glass right in front of my face.

I yelled at my lieutenant, "Doc, we have to go!"

"What?" Between the commotion of the crowd and his efforts to get the most reasonable price for ice, he had no idea what had just occurred.

I yelled at him again, louder.

I looked to my right at all these children and I thought, If anything happens, who am I going to shoot? I can't shoot these kids.

Visions flashed through my mind of the two of us being pulled from the vehicle and beaten to death. We would be helpless to do anything. So I started yelling, "Doc! We have to get out of here!"

At that point he noticed the panic in my voice and the crack in the window and started speeding off.

Later, he said we couldn't tell anyone what had transpired because we had broken so many rules. Not only weren't we supposed to be buying anything, we weren't even supposed to be off post.

For the next week and a half I was too mad to go anyplace with him, even though I knew I could get an article fifteen for refusing.

But my lieutenant didn't make a stink about it because he didn't want to have to explain my reasons to anyone; he just sat around drinking his sodas and waiting for me to get over it.

Leslie Watson
U.S. Army

# FIFTY-ONE

*"There never was a time when, in my opinion,*
*some way could not be found to prevent the drawing of the sword."*
General Ulysses S. Grant

Major Liesl R. Carter began flying lessons at the age of sixteen. In 1993 she graduated from the Air Force Academy, and has been flying the KC-135 Stratotanker for the past ten years. Her supportive husband is a stay-at-home dad for their young son, Maxwell.

## IT'S NOT ABOUT STYLE

I feel privileged to be a KC-135 pilot, and I am passionate about my job. I think it is phenomenal that the Air Force offers this extraordinary training to so many young people.

Another great thing about the Air Force, and particularly my crew, is that being a woman is no big deal, it's just so normal. A funny example of this is a conversation I had with a friend of mine, who told me that while she was on a recent flight with an all-female crew, they refueled off another "unmanned" aircraft.

Throughout my military career I've been treated wonderfully. I've never experienced any kind of discrimination, not even during pregnancy.

For a pilot, the standard uniform is a flightsuit. This jumpsuit is made of a flame-resistant fabric called nomex, in an olive drab shade of green with zippered pockets and a zipper down the front. It's like putting your pajamas on to go to work.

There are also two styles of maternity uniforms. The first consists of a light blue parachute-shaped shirt and polyester pants. The second is a camouflage battle dress uniform, which is either a very funny name or a very appropriate one depending on your perspective.

Both styles are even less fashionable than the flightsuit, however, and while pregnant with my first child, I didn't want to wear either one until I had to. But because I was able to fly during my second trimester, I had to change flightsuit sizes twice in the first six months in order to accommodate my growing belly.

I hadn't realized how big I had gotten. But I knew it was time to switch uniforms when I overheard a young boom operator asking one of the other booms, "Is Major Carter pregnant, or is she just getting fat?"

On the afternoon of Saturday, October 2, 2004, miserable and four days overdue with my son, my husband and I took a two-mile hike. Within two hours of returning home, I went into labor.

By eleven o'clock that evening my contractions were two to three minutes apart, so we grabbed my bag and headed for the car. Stationed with the United States Air Force at RAF Mildenhall, United Kingdom, we were twenty minutes away from the nearest hospital, on Lakenheath Royal Air Force Base.

By the time we got to the gate my pain was constant. To make matters worse, instead of waving us through the security police gestured for us to go to the vehicle search area.

"You have got to be kidding me," I said to my husband.

He pulled over, rolled down the window and told the airman we were on our way to the hospital for labor and delivery.

Before the airman could answer I leaned over, and in a voice my husband still swears came from *The Exorcist* said, "I am not getting out of the car!"

The airman's eyes widened as he looked from me to my husband. "Okay," he said as he waved us through the gate. "Works for me!"

Our son, Maxwell, was born nearly twelve hours later.

Major Liesl R. Carter
U.S. Air Force

# FIFTY-TWO

*"I am a soldier, I fight where I am told, and I win where I fight."*
General George Patton, Jr.

India Roderick joined the Coast Guard in 1990. During her nine-year enlistment, she married a coastie and was pregnant for every major move. She experienced many adventures, and served for nearly three years aboard the 270-foot cutter *Northland*. Currently, she is pursuing a degree in behavioral science.

## A LOT OF FUSS ABOUT NOTHING

One day, while stationed on the Coast Guard Cutter *Northland* and on a northern patrol, I took a boarding team over to a boat for a fishery inspection in our nineteen-foot inflatable.

While our ship went to investigate another fishing boat about a mile away, my instructions as driver were to stay on site, along with my engineer and the team.

Because of the law enforcement nature of our mission, we wore bulletproof vests beneath our life jackets in case we met with resistance, so we were bulkier and heavier than normal and sat pretty low to the water. So even though the cutter wasn't a great distance from us, as it motored away it was soon completely out of our sight.

About two hours later, the boarding team had gathered and was ready to leave the fishing boat. The inspection had gone well, and the fishing crew had been very receptive and cooperative.

Once the team was back on our boat, the fishing vessel began traveling north so they could get back to their task of fishing. Alone now in the middle of the immense ocean, we suddenly felt very small and vulnerable.

Our ship had gone east of our original position, so I pointed the RHI due east and started making our way. Though the ship remained out of our sight we had radio communications, and soon the ship answered, assuring us they were just over the horizon and had us clearly on their radar.

Thank goodness.

Just when we caught a glimpse of the ship and were breathing a little easier, the officer of the deck called us from the pilothouse. "Need to inform you," he said, "that halfway between you and the ship, an extremely large shark is close to the surface."

The radio on the RHI is actually a handheld with the mike clipped to my lifejacket on my right shoulder area. In this position I could hear it better over the noise of the boat, and I could just reach up and hit the button to talk.

But everyone else could hear it as well, and the tension level skyrocketed. If we had been inside it would have blown the roof off. Everyone tightened their grips on their respective handholds and scooted to a less comfortable but safer position toward the center, and I could feel the boat shake. Fortunately the controls weren't foot-operated, since my legs were now pinned to the side of my seat.

Because slowing down would prolong the agony, and speeding up would increase the risk, I maintained my course and speed. Just before the officer's announcement, I, too, had caught a glimpse of something near the surface of the water in the general vicinity he had referred. It hadn't seemed to be moving on its own, but I had already decided to stay clear of that proximity – until the officer ordered me to go to that exact spot.

"I want you to give me a confirmation of what is at the water's surface," he said, "about 500 meters off our port side."

What the hell was he thinking? "Sir, are you sure this is needed right now?" Although I tried to be respectful, in my mind I threw bricks. "Affirmative! I need confirmation."

Someone on the RHI said, "Don't worry, we can handle this. We know how to swim, and we have weapons."

Agreement came in a round of grunts. These guys weren't going to show an ounce of fear to a woman. In addition, we now had the ship in our sight, and a decent-sized crowd had gathered to watch.

We approached the object and circled it at wide berth.

It looked like a log, so we made a second pass.

It was a log! In fact it was a tree floating in the water.

Breathing easier, we passed on the news that no shark had been found, and returned to the ship.

By the time the RHI had been put away and I had finished my immediate duties, the watch had switched over. But I found the previous officer of the deck still on the bridge and requested a word with him.

"With all due respect, sir, we couldn't have done anything about a monster shark." I tried to stay calm, because he did outrank me. "And by telling me about it, you put the whole boat crew in danger."

He had already received some ribbing on the bridge, and in addition to being defensive he showed no sign of backing down. "I know it was a giant shark," he said. "I just know it."

"Okay." I shook my head, remembering why I had never given him any points for super-intelligence. "But next time, please do us all a favor and keep it to yourself."

India Roderick
U.S. Coast Guard

# FIFTY-THREE

*"A leader is a man who can adapt principles to circumstances."*
General George Patton, Jr.

Colonel Robyn M. King embarked on her Air Force career in 1981. She has always strived to work hard, be herself, and reach down and bring others along on the journey. Over the course of her career, she has been a mentor and leader to thousands of cadets.

## JUST TRYING TO BE ME

I received my commission as a second lieutenant after many doors and windows had already been opened for young women. Not only had the first class of female Air Force grads been in the field for six months, but also, Major General Norma Brown pinned on one of my bars, as she happened to be at my ceremony.

Now, as I look back almost twenty-six years later, I feel most fortunate to have had the career I've had, despite the lack of any significant male role models or career mentors. My mother, my true mentor and hero, taught me from a very early age that I could do anything if I put my mind to it. She had the courage to divorce my abusive father back in 1965 when I was eight years old, a huge move for a woman to make in that time period, especially in a small town.

When I went into the service, women still competed amongst themselves for recognition and acceptance. As a result, they were very hesitant to reach down and bring the rest of us along on the journey. I resent them for that, as a large aspect of leadership is mentoring and developing those who will eventually replace us.

As a female 0-6 with a Ph.D. who's spent the majority of her career outside mainstream academia, I sometimes forget I possess a lot of insight and wisdom that I need to impart to others before I depart.

One of my favorite sayings is inscribed on a peregrine falcon statue, given to me by my Cadet Group when I left my position at the United States Air Force Academy: *A true measure of leadership is the success of your people.*

An example of this is one of my most cherished "take-aways" from the academy, and involves one of my female problem children, "Suzy Q." Though beautiful, smart, and ambitious – the ideal poster child for a USAFA grad – she was also a rebel of sorts, and it got her into enough trouble to ultimately save herself, so to speak.

After she lipped off in my presence during a routine uniform inspection early in her senior year, I decided to make her my special project. We'd meet occasionally for mentoring sessions, and she was well on her way to graduation with her class in late May 2001, and then on to selectively-manned intelligence training. But two weeks before graduation she got arrested downtown for being drunk and disorderly, and I had to make her a late grad and keep her at the academy until August of that year.

Consequently, she graduated by herself, devoid of the fanfare enjoyed earlier by her more than 950 classmates. Because of her late graduation and the alcohol incident, her security clearance was delayed, and held up once again when it got caught up in the anthrax mail in the Washington D.C. area. Subsequently, she worked on staff at the Intel school for several months, did extremely well, and began to build up career accolades.

Since then, she has been an ace performer, married a wonderful Air Force pilot and is expecting her first child next month. She's often told me that even today she reflects on the things I used to tell her, and that she deeply appreciates the patience and compassion I extended.

To this day I love her like a daughter, and will always look back on that particular aspect of my job as one of the things I'm most proud of.

Over the years, I have encountered good examples of what not to be. In fact, I can safely say my three worst bosses were women. The first one was simply intimidated by me because I could beat her on the golf course. The second wanted me to be her best friend because she was single and lonely. And the third was my notorious boss at USAFA, who got caught up in the firing frenzy and thought she had to abuse and intimidate people in order for them to respond to her.

Through it all, I've just tried to be myself. After all, that's all I've ever known who to be, for better or worse. Sometimes that means being a little rough around the edges. But always it means caring for the people who work for you and knowing *that* is *not* a sign of weakness.

I've tried to keep my competitive edge in check, although it was ingrained in me as a tomboy, a high school and college athlete, and the fact I am a true Type A personality. And I've learned to embrace the TEAM (Together Everyone Achieves More) concept.

My efforts have paid off hugely, as my mission support squadron at Holloman during my tenure as commander won more MAJCOM and AF-level awards than any other unit in history. It wasn't because of my leadership per se, but because I had great people I cared about. I allowed them to run their areas as they saw fit, stepped in when I needed to, and didn't let them settle for anything less than what they deserved.

I tried to take care of my people and they definitely took care of the mission.

I've never felt like I've been held back in the Air Force because I am a woman. Maybe due to the reason the doors had already been blasted open, or the fact I've served in a support function where women are numerous. Or, perhaps it's because I refused to be treated as a second-class citizen, and always tried to be ultra-competent so people would respect my work first, and my position or gender second. Or possibly, it's because I've always been able to relate to men on their level, whether we're talking about sports or home improvement projects.

One thing I know for sure, however, is that the environment toward female cadets at USAFA sickened me during my tenure there. Despite the fact this is the twenty-first century, nearly twenty per cent of the cadet population believed women didn't belong in the military.

In 2003, dozens of women came forward with allegations of rape and sexual assault that occurred at the academy over the years. While the whole sexual assault scandal was extremely painful, it did bring to the limelight a culture desperately in need of changing its views toward women. I do believe the seeds have been planted, though, and we should see a significant difference in the environment there over the next few years.

I would say a combination of life and career events has molded who I am and how I approach my profession. The first of these occurred during my first two years of active duty, when I was wrongly accused of drug and homosexuality charges and faced discharge from the Air Force. The situation lasted almost eighteen months and was obviously resolved in my favor.

My mother, who always believed in me, told me if I could survive that I could survive anything. And she was right. It made me far more confident in myself and gave me a different perspective on military discipline – ensuring I had *all* the facts before punishing someone.

The second event was the sexual scandal at USAFA. One day I looked around and realized everyone above me in the chain of command had been fired, and I was the continuity for the new team. Despite public assurances by the Secretary and the Chief of Staff of the Air Force that no actions would be taken until all investigations were complete, all five senior officers were gone within a month's time.

When the SECAF and CSAF caved into political pressure and went back on their word, I lost a lot of faith in the Air Force. As a result, I have a deeper appreciation for the role that politics and the media play in our national defense.

The third and final event is ongoing right now. My mother had back surgery in August 2005, followed by one catastrophic setback after another. As she's been my role model and best friend, my biggest fear in life is losing her.

Now, I'm facing that fear – alone.

But I haven't completely crumbled. And I will survive this, even if she doesn't. Because I am a woman with strength and independence – just like my mother.

Colonel Robyn M. King
U.S. Air Force

# FIFTY-FOUR

*"Be convinced that to be happy means to be free*
*and that to be free means to be brave."*
Thucydides

Commander Kay L. Hartzell served with the Coast Guard from 1973 to 1993, where a strong work ethic and sense of humor saw her through the tough times. In 1979, she became the first woman to command a Coast Guard station. Since her retirement, she has traveled extensively with family and friends.

## BRASS BALLS TO TIARAS

While stationed at Headquarters, I was in charge of the Coast Guard nationwide enlisted recruiting program. The position offered lots of opportunities for travel and interaction with my enlisted recruiters.

During this assignment, I finally met some of the other female officers I had only heard about or spoken with on the phone. Foolishly, the Coast Guard had assigned most of the senior female officers to Headquarters at the same time, and we quickly bonded.

Unfortunately, the timing coincided with a major study to track women in the Coast Guard, so all eyes were suddenly focused on us. If two or more of us met in a hallway, we were asked if we were having a union meeting. In fact, we were constantly accused of conspiring – not that two males together were ever seen as a conspiracy, but what do I know!

Parking at Headquarters was extremely difficult. But next door, a Park Service marina rented spaces for folks who moored boats there. Most people didn't rent a parking slip, so there were a number of spaces available – provided you knew of someone leaving.

When the ex-husband of one of my female cohorts had to give up his space due to a transfer, she put out the parking lot alert, and we all hustled down to claim our spots.

Once our parking spaces were confirmed, one of our intrepid folks wandered around the marina and discovered a building with a beer machine. Lordy, lordy – we had a spot to meet. The paranoia within our own building had become unbearable, and we really needed a refuge.

In the beginning, all of us with parking spots had a K in our names, and I came up with the moniker of ARK, for the Association of Rowdy Kays. Plus, Ark meant a place of refuge. Most of us had window offices that overlooked the building, so we devised various signals – a lantern in a window, or smoke from the wood stove meant the Ark was in session, and folks could come down.

Whenever we were having a bad day, we would simply leave phone messages that said "ARK!" We did allow a few trusted male friends into our circle, but otherwise it was our girl's playhouse. We had pizzas and other foods delivered while waiting to respond to congressional questions, and waited out torrential downpours before going home. But most of all we bonded, had fun, and developed lifelong friendships.

The spirit of the ARK continues today with the Brass Tiaras. When I retired in 1993, my new friends put on a wonderful surprise retirement party. In the fall of 1994, another member retired, and six of us met for a week at a timeshare in Virginia. We had a terrific time, and decided we should meet again.

While driving about the wine fields, I thought we should come up with a name for our group. We thought up words that had been used against us – princesses, comes to mind – as well as the strengths we needed to succeed – brass balls is a typical nautical description. And once we started free thinking in those terms, we remembered an optional uniform piece – a beaded tiara – that none of us would ever be caught wearing, much less buying. So the club name became obvious – The Brass Tiaras – or BTs for short.

In the past twelve years we have traveled from Europe to French Polynesia. We've had a marvelous time, and our numbers continue to expand. Two of our most remarkable trips were to Europe. In 1998, in honor of my fiftieth, I rented two, fifty-foot self-drive boats that we navigated down the Burgundy Canal and the Saone River. We began our trip in Paris, trained to Dijon where we picked up the boats, and ended off at the Saone.

We then trained to Munich, by way of Strasbourg, and spent four days at Oktoberfest. What a trip!

The second excursion was three years ago when I rented a medieval palace outside of Siena, and apartments in Positano and Rome. We had such a good time that I am duplicating some parts of the trip for this October. We'll again have our twelve bedroom, thirteen-bath *palazzo*, plus apartments in Rome and Venice.

Two months from tonight I will be ensconced in a Roman apartment adjacent to the *Campo de Fiori*. I can't wait!

Commander Kay L. Hartzell, (retired)
U.S. Coast Guard

# FIFTY-FIVE

*"The best luck of all is the luck you make for yourself."*
General Douglas MacArthur

Captain Melissa A. Torres began her military career with the Army in 1988. Today she is nearing retirement as a member of the Montana Army National Guard. She is a biathlete and entrepreneur, who loves gardening and gourmet cooking.

## MARCHING ON

At the age of twenty-two, desperate for direction and a challenge in life, I joined the Army as a combat medical specialist, and attended basic training at Fort Jackson, South Carolina. I couldn't get over the trees and scenery that varied so much from my home in Phoenix, Arizona.

While stationed at Fort Lewis, Washington, with the 9th Division Artillery, I served as a medic with the trauma treatment team. I was the only female gun medic.

In 1993, I joined the Montana Army National Guard, where I fueled OH-58s, UH-1s and Cobra helicopters in subzero temperatures while waiting for a slot to open up as a flight medic. I never knew it could get so cold! Thankfully I only did a few months of that before I moved into a flight slot.

There are few females in the aviation world in Montana unless they are flight operations. Every time we get a female to flight school they love the experience so much they end up being wooed by the active Army, making it difficult for women to prove their ability to hold National Guard positions historically held by men – or so I thought.

I held that position as an E-5 with male E-6's working for me. I felt surrounded by older brothers with a dialect all our own. These men cheered me on through college as a single mother working myself to the bone. And encouraged me to pursue law school, and flight school – until they found out my age.

Like families, we had the ability to laugh at ourselves like kids. I remember being left outside to tie down rotor systems on aircraft, which at my size, 5' 4" and 115 lbs. on a good day, was no easy task. One day, I had to cover the exhaust of a turbine engine helicopter and needed a pilot to give me a boost. When he walked away, thinking I was done and on the ground, he turned to find me dangling by the front of my coat from a hook on the side of the aircraft. Another time, I was hoisted into a field recently inhabited by cattle. Needless to say, once back in the aircraft we were doors open all the way home!

Because I had performed NTC (National Training Center) rotations in the active Army, I was asked to head up the aid station. These men were so amazing and the best medics I have ever worked with. Egos never got in the way of our decision-making and teamwork. When they saw me stumble they were the first to help and were always open to my leadership and suggestions.

The only reason I bring up men working for me is that they could have all turned on me and waited for me to fail. But we held each other together in stressful times, during real life aero-medevacs, and I helped them understand mass casualty ops, and where and what the OPFOR (opposing forces) was up to.

In 2000, I received a direct commission for time in service and performance. The second soldier to benefit from this new policy, I had to deal with all the controversial fall-out.

In the military, women face trials and discrimination mostly due to the fact we aren't always considered to be as strong or as capable as our counterparts. Nowadays, though, more men are educated in our struggles and are encouraging us to move into places we may not have been before.

Although I've faced my share of obstacles and had to prove myself able, as a woman I probably would have had the same hardships in the corporate civilian world, so I don't want the military to be highlighted as chauvinistic. We are, in fact, the only organization without the glass ceiling when it comes to pay and benefits. As a captain, I make the same as any other captain – male or female.

Today, I feel I am successful in my life because of some incredible men I have known. From my father to the pilots, crew chiefs, gun bunnies, infantrymen, general officers, and all the other men I have had the pleasure of working with, I owe a debt of gratitude.

Over the years, I've had some amazing jobs and experiences. Although illness will prevent me from extending my career to the age of sixty, I've had a great ride. I have lunched with WWII veterans who fought on Normandy's beaches; sat on Air Force 2, at the desk of the vice president; escorted the first African-American

Airborne unit, the Triple Nickels; and toured the Women's memorial in Washington D.C. with the founder, Brigadier General Wilma Vaught. In addition, I have trained many soldiers in aero-medevac rescue and hoist.

I also had the opportunity to be one of the motivational forces in creating and taking a program called Challenge through the state legislature. State and federally funded, this highly successful volunteer program is geared to helping teenagers finish high school and move on to college, vocational training, or the military, and is followed by a year of mentoring.

Because of the confidence and strength I have gained from the military, I strive to take all the opportunities that come my way. In 2002, I joined the Montana National Guard summer biathlon team, and placed first, second, and third in the Nationals at Yellowstone, only nine months after the birth of my son.

In my eighteen-year career, I have gained the skill to stand my ground, carefully assess a situation, and not second-guess myself.

I have learned to march on, and never give up.

Captain Melissa A. Torres
Army National Guard

# FIFTY-SIX

*" . . . without a respectable Navy, alas America!"*
Captain John Paul Jones

Petty Officer Mary West joined the Air Force in 1979, and the Navy in 1996. She is a recruiter, and a first-time grandmother who enjoys drawing, painting with oils, and researching her family history.

## MAKING A DIFFERENCE

When I graduated from high school, I wanted to go to college and study Wild Life Management and Forestry Technology. But like most kids, I didn't have the money.

Although I'd grown up at the tail end of the hippie era listening to "anti-establishment" ideas, I decided to join the Navy. The education benefits were enticing, as was a growing desire to follow in my dad's footsteps.

Unfortunately, the Navy couldn't get me into school for eighteen months, and I needed a job. Young and impatient, I wanted to leave sooner. I said as much, and as it turned out an Air Force

241

recruiter in earshot told me he had a recruit who had fallen out. Therefore he had a slot to fill.

When he said, "I can get you out of here tomorrow," I said, "Okay!"

So I joined the U.S. Air Force in 1979, as a liquid fuels maintenance technician.

I went to boot camp in San Antonio, Texas, and then on to Chanute AFB, Illinois, for training, where I spent about ten weeks learning how to be responsible for the maintenance of fuel pipelines and storage tanks. I went inside fuel storage tanks big enough to hold two four-bedroom houses.

While in Illinois, I got a tattoo. I had made friends with three other girls, and we all wanted to get one alike so we could bond ourselves together as sisters. We picked a sunset tattoo, and mine is on the right side of my upper back, toward my shoulder.

When I completed training, I went to Seymour Johnson, AFB, North Carolina, and then on to Germany for three years. I really enjoyed it there. During that time I saw almost all of Europe, and learned about the people, culture, food and wine.

Following my tour in Germany, I spent three years at MacDill AFB, in Tampa, Florida, where I decided I wanted to change jobs. I did everything necessary, but my requests were repeatedly denied. Finally I asked, "What else can I do?"

Up for re-enlistment, I learned I could change military branches. So I went home and discussed the situation with my dad. "Well," he said, "you started out trying to go Navy. Why don't you give it another shot?"

I called a Navy recruiter and set up an appointment. I told him I wanted some type of nursing job. He said that was a corpsman position, which is very similar to an LPN, and he could help me with that. Therefore, I enlisted in the Navy in 1996, and went to Bremerton Washington Hospital where I received training in OB-GYN and thermal burns.

From Washington, I went to the Naval and Marine Corps Reserve Center in Salt Lake City, Utah. There, I put in an application to be a recruiter, went to New Orleans for a three-week recruiter course, and started recruiting.

Among other reasons, I chose a recruiting job because I believe what the Navy has to offer – money, education, and medical/dental benefits – can assist a lot of people. In addition, I could stay in a single spot for a length of time.

I have been recruiting now for six years. It is a difficult job, however, as we have quotas to meet – currently it is one recruit per month – and lots of stress. But I do love the opportunity to meet so many different kinds of people. Although most of them sign up for the money, school benefits, travel opportunities, or even to escape parents or significant others, I really enjoy and admire the patriotic ones – because the bonus money isn't as important to them as their desire to serve their country.

Another reason I like my job is because I get to watch a lot of young people grow and excel. I even had the privilege of seeing the very first person I put in receive his commission as an officer. That was something special for me. It feels good to know I can make a difference in someone's life.

Being the first woman in my shop was challenging. But with a little work and communication I was able to adapt. I remember one occasion where I wanted to be one of the guys and I started talking like "a sailor." An older military man told me I could still be one of the guys without talking like them. In other words, I was reminded that women can hold what is traditionally a man's job and still be feminine.

In three years, I hope to retire. After a long and satisfying military career I look forward to a change. Besides, I am a grandma now, and I can't wait to spend more time with my family.

Petty Officer First Class Mary West
U.S. Navy

# FIFTY-SEVEN

*"There is no security in this life. There is only opportunity."*
General Douglas MacArthur

Port Security Chief Maxine Cavanaugh began her military career with the Marine Corps in 1956. Twenty years later she joined the Coast Guard Reserve, where she served as a member of the 1984 Olympics Task Force; was selected as USCG Reserve Petty Officer of the Year by Naval Enlisted Reserve Association; taught two summers at the Reserve Training Center at Yorktown, Virginia; and spent a year on active duty as assistant to the Women's Policy Advisor. A member of the Coast Guard Auxiliary, she now writes for FEMA in the Public Affairs cadre, and deploys when needed for federal disasters. In 2004, she and her daughter made Coast Guard history as the first mother-daughter team of Chief Petty Officers.

## SHE CALLED ME CHIEF MOM

A year out of high school and dissatisfied with my job, I joined the Marine Corps, and left Columbia, Missouri, to attend boot camp at Parris Island, South Carolina. There, I promptly fell and broke both wrists while running backward relay races.

After two months in the hospital, I completed basic training and was assigned to Camp Lejeune, North Carolina. Inside a year, I accepted an opportunity to be stationed in Hawaii, where I met and married my husband and took my discharge, which at the time was available to women who didn't have any training to make up after marriage.

Nearly twenty years later and divorced, I responded to an ad for the Coast Guard Reserve, where I eventually wound up in Port Security, and advanced up the ladder making Chief Petty Officer in minimal time. During this time frame, I also recruited my daughter, Grace, a high school junior, into the Reserve.

When Grace came into my Port Security unit, immediate concern arose that there might be bias if any tricky situation arose. But nothing was ever mentioned to a fellow reservist who had recruited his two sons into our unit, or about the fact that they were all in the same chain of command.

For the most part, being in the same unit was a good experience. I gave Grace the benefit of my knowledge, we worked to keep mother and daughter on separate teams, and we always did our best to be professional in our Reserve relationship – with one exception: she called me Chief Mom.

While serving in the same Port Security unit as two of only four women, one year we worked with the Army Reserve to learn riot and crowd control. The following year we were invited to work with them again and play the role of protesters.

When Grace arrived at the pier where everyone had assembled, our guys did a double take. "Grace, what's this? Are you really pregnant?"

My daughter, always one with unique ideas, had come up with a scenario to help the Army Reservists deal with unanticipated situations. She had borrowed maternity clothes from a college classmate, stuffed a soccer ball into her pantyhose and gone to meet our fellow reservists who were participating in the exercise.

At the Army training center it was time for the Army to do the double take as Coast Guard reservists piled out of their van, solicitous of the "pregnant protester."

The Coast Guard reservists played their roles well, helping the only woman among the protesters as needed, even joining in a sit-in and other protesting activities. It was a successful day, with the Army Reserve learning to expect the unexpected. They hadn't even provided for female restrooms!

Then came Desert Shield/Desert Storm, and some of our unit members were activated. I was in my last semester in graduate school taking a required course only offered in alternate semesters, but Grace had just graduated from the University of Hawaii. Activated to go to Guam and supervise the loading of ammunition on Navy ships, she had three days to notify her employers and get her affairs in order.

Grace had been working four jobs to save up to go to the mainland, as Hawaii just didn't offer much in the way of jobs to keep its young people at home. And when she returned home after nearly three months on active duty, she decided to make the Coast Guard her full-time job.

About the time I finished grad school, a temporary position became available at Headquarters in Washington, D.C., and I, too, accepted full-time employment with the Coast Guard. I spent the next year as assistant to the Women's Policy Advisor working on recruitment and retention problems; helping set policy regarding women, i.e. accommodations on ships, etc.; and was responsible for a toll free number that both men and women could call and discuss problems or situations.

Grace changed rates to go active duty and took her new training at Yorktown. Over the Christmas holidays I helped her drive across the States to her new assignment on a ship out of Seattle.

Although I retired in 1996, Grace continued in her rate, married, and co-located with her coastie husband to the San Francisco Bay area. When she advanced to Chief, he was on patrol with his ship, and I flew to San Francisco to attend the traditional Chiefs initiation.

The ceremony, performed on the flight deck of the HORNET, a decommissioned aircraft carrier, culminated with the official pinning on of the anchors. I had given Grace some of my anchors when the list came out with her name on it. And as I pinned one of those on my daughter, the next generation of Coast Guard chiefs, there wasn't a dry eye between us. As mother and daughter Coast Guard Chief Petty Officers, we had set a new tradition.

Port Security Chief Maxine Cavanaugh, (retired)
U.S. Coast Guard

# FIFTY-EIGHT

*"You must do your damnedest and win."*
General George Patton, Jr.

Chief Warrant Officer Kayce C. Lowry is a Blackhawk pilot who began her career with the Army National Guard in 1999. She enjoys hiking, basketball, riding four-wheelers, and being with friends and family. When she retires from the military, she would like to fly helicopters for the Forest Service.

## THE BEST JOB I COULD ASK FOR

My father missed the event of my birth, as he had just begun a career in the military and could not get away from his duties. But little did he know that his daughter would one day follow in his footsteps.

As a child I liked to dress up like my dad, wearing his boots and hat. These antics eventually earned me the nickname Combat Kayce. Later, when I was a junior in high school trying to figure out what I wanted to do with my life and wondering how I would pay for college, my father opened a whole new window for me by asking me if I would like to go to flight school.

A pilot himself, as well as head of recruiting and retention for the Utah National Guard, he provided me with all the insight he could. Aware of the good and bad aspects of a military career, I contemplated the best course of action for my life and joined the Guard with the consent and signature of my parents at the age of seventeen, on the 9th day of August, 1999. As my recruiter my father had the honor of swearing me in, and the day was filled with excitement and anxiety. I had actually done it!

With one year of high school remaining I had opted to enlist under the delayed entry program. That way I could finish school, perform my obligation of one weekend a month and two weeks of training a year, and then ship out for boot camp the summer following graduation.

My senior year flew by. Graduation came and went, and then it was time to get down to business. In September, I left for Fort Sill, Oklahoma – alone, barely eighteen, and on my first flight.

I arrived at Fort Sill with no idea of what to expect. A bus waited for me at the airport with a very large drill sergeant as driver. Though scared to death, somehow that feeling didn't last long due to all the screaming and yelling going on, or the fact that they kept us so busy I didn't have time to think about it.

On my first day I tried my best to outdo the other females. I guess it paid off because I had a six-foot five-inch drill sergeant come up to me, get in my face, and tell me to remember his face because I was going to be in his platoon whether I liked it or not.

The first few weeks I acted as assistant platoon guide. And when our platoon guide got fired for not allowing a soldier to eat, I became platoon guide for the remainder of the course. I didn't mind the responsibility but I did mind the lack of sleep.

As platoon guide in charge of sixty-three soldiers, including fifteen women, every problem each soldier had was mine to resolve and take care of.

The drill sergeants worked directly with me, giving me instructions of what needed to be done for the day. It was then up to me to ensure all tasks were completed to the standard. Being platoon guide, of course, had a downside, as I got blamed for anything that went wrong, took the heat for my soldiers, and acted as buffer between drill sergeants and privates. That was the beginning of my leadership career, however, and an experience I will never forget.

After basic training I went directly to Fort Gordon, Georgia, for Advanced Individual Training (AIT) as a 31U communications specialist. It was a step up from basic training, not as much yelling, and a little more freedom. I loved every minute of it.

By April of 2001 I had returned home, a trained fighting machine, unaware of my unit's agenda. The 1-211th Attack Aviation Battalion would leave for Kuwait in July. The excitement set in again. I was actually going to deploy and be able to use my new skills.

On our way to Kuwait, our C-5 broke down in Rota, Spain, where we wound up spending four unexpected days filled with pure sunshine and delight. Then we were off to sandy Kuwait, where we arrived around two o'clock in the morning, and were hit with a rush of hot air and temperatures of 110 degrees when we stepped off the plane.

Kuwait was nothing like I had expected. In fact, I was pretty impressed by the modern capital. What did not impress me, though, were views toward females, and the fact that every time I went to town I had to be accompanied by a group of men, who had to do just about everything for me because of my sex. I hated not being able to just go and do as I pleased. It was humiliating.

There were about ten women in my unit, and we stayed in warehouses that had been converted into barracks, with two-man rooms.

My main duty was to provide a retrans site whenever needed. Retrans is a spot out on the highest point we can get to, where two radios are set up in order to boost the signal further so the aircraft or convoy can go a greater distance and not lose communications with the home base. Sometimes I got to go out to the FARPS (Forward Arming and Refueling Site) to help with the communications and radios there.

The scariest time of my deployment was September 11, 2001. I felt so helpless being stuck in a country halfway around the world while the United States was under attack. Worrying about my family and the possibility of multiple attacks left me feeling afraid and useless. And watching the footage on television time after time overwhelmed me with the worst feelings of my life.

From that point on we were no longer allowed to go off post, and we had to carry our equipment with us at all times.

Seven months later, we were on our way home.

I started working full time, trying to save money to start college. I put together my packet and applied for flight school. During this time I met my supportive husband, Jeremy. His friends and family thought he was crazy to date a military girl. At first even he wasn't quite sure what to think about it, especially when I assured him that nothing would keep me from going to flight school – not even marriage.

He finally accepted that fact and we got married in December of 2002. The following July, I left for Fort Rucker, Alabama, to attend Warrant Officer Candidate Course (WOCC).

WOCC turned out to be the longest six weeks of my life. It was extremely challenging, both mentally and physically. A typical day began with a 0500 wake up call, followed by seven minutes to get your bunk made, your teeth brushed, your shoes and socks on, your wall locker displayed correctly, go to the bathroom and be down in front of your building for formation. The fact that there were sixty-five soldiers doing this at once didn't make things any easier.

Once we were in formation, we had to take accountability and start stretching for our exercises. We would work out for forty-five minutes or so, which included a five or six-mile run, pushups and sit-ups. We then had twenty minutes to get everyone showered and dressed, and clean the barracks.

Because there were only two women in my class, we had to shower before everyone else, which meant we had to hurry that much faster.

As soon as we were all cleaned up, we went down to formation and headed to chow. At chow, we had to wait until our table was full before we could sit down. Once you were down, there was no talking and it was a square meal. You could only take one bite at a time and you had to finish that bite before you could take another.

After chow, we were marched to class where we spent the rest of the day trying to stay awake and listen to the instructors.

And then it started all over again. The "no time for anything" never ended.

As soon as I finished WOCC, I went directly to flight school, also held at Fort Rucker, and my husband came to stay with me for the duration of training.

There were fifty people in my class. I was the only female for the first six months, and then two more joined us. My stick buddy, or flying partner, had graduated from West Point with a four-year degree in engineering, and his example strengthened my goal to attend college. We got along great.

One year and two months later I had completed training and qualified as a Blackhawk helicopter pilot. Flight school was the best thing I have ever accomplished. To me, nothing feels better than completing a goal.

The purpose of the Blackhawk is to move things or people. We do all kinds of movement missions. We fight forest fires, take paratroopers, fly VIPs, haul equipment, and provide medevac. It just depends on the need at the time.

It is a pretty big aircraft – around fifty-three feet long with a capacity of 22,000 pounds. Troop capacity depends on the configuration we have at the time, but we can take up to fourteen people in seats, or remove the seats and take paratroopers, equipment, or be set up for medevac and make room for stretchers.

Because things can get really busy in the cockpit, the Blackhawk is a dual pilot aircraft. Pilots have to have a working knowledge of the switches, and have all kinds of things memorized such as emergency procedures and limitations of the aircraft. It's a lot of information, and we have to study nearly every day just to keep things fresh in our minds.

This time when I returned to my unit I discovered we were going to Nicaragua. We had been tasked with supporting a humanitarian mission called New Horizons, going there to build schools and churches. Imagine my excitement. Just back from flight school with the opportunity to fly in a foreign country.

We went down on three-week rotations. Because I volunteered to do multiple ones, I stayed there six amazing weeks. The people were friendly, I saw some of the most beautiful sunsets, and the country, with volcanic sand coal black amongst all the greenery, was incredible.

While providing medevac support to ground crews, we flew at an altitude of about twenty-five feet through mountains, next to volcanoes, and out over the sea. On my first flight out to the ocean, we were flying along when all of a sudden the ground dropped out from under us, and we were over a huge cliff that met the water. It was one of the most exciting moments I have experienced.

Although I was the only female there with the Blackhawk Company, the men I work with are great. They treat me as an equal, and appreciate the fact that I can hold my own without flaking out on them.

A full-time employee of the National Guard, I am S-1, or Human Resource Officer for the 2-211th General Support Aviation Battalion during the week, and TACOPS, or Tactical Operations Officer and a pilot on weekends. As a pilot, I have to maintain close to one hundred hours a year, so as long as my full-time job is done to the standard, I get to fly during the week as well.

Words cannot express the passion I have for my job. It is the most incredible feeling to be in the air and see the world from a different view. The military has blessed my life and given me countless opportunities. It is the best job I could ask for.

Chief Warrant Officer Two Kayce C. Lowry
Army National Guard

# FIFTY-NINE

*"It is foolish and wrong to mourn the men who died.*
*Rather we should thank God that such men lived."*
General George Patton, Jr.

Marine Science Technician Jayne Anne Tragesser never expected to survive Army boot camp, only to suffer through another one when she joined the Coast Guard several years later. As a coastie, she is proud of her job and country, and would like to encourage all women in today's military to take the opportunity to speak with older servicewomen and veterans.

## MY PERSONAL HERO

I met my personal hero while stationed in Alexandria, Virginia, with the United States Coast Guard Honor Guard. At the time, I was one of four women out of sixty-three members.

The Honor Guard provides presidential support duty to the Military District of Washington, and ceremonial jobs at the Pentagon, White House, Arlington National Cemetery, and other venues.

One Friday afternoon in January as I prepared to leave the office, a last-second request came in from Coast Guard Decedent Affairs, Washington D.C., for a coastie to do a flag fold/presentation at a funeral that Saturday, for Lieutenant Commander Eugena Hartman, a Coast Guard SPAR.

In the World War II era, women were allowed to serve in administration, nursing, and general services to free up men to fight on the fronts. In the Coast Guard, this division was called SPARs, named after the Coast Guard motto, *Semper Paratus,* or Always Ready, and its members paved the way for women in the military today.

We did funerals all the time for retired coasties in Arlington National Cemetery. But this opportunity really hit home. Like the suffragettes who fought for seventy years for women's right to vote, this woman had been a pioneer for servicewomen – a suffragist in her own right.

As I prepared for the ceremony, never before had I worked so hard pressing out my uniform, shining my heel brass and medals, and ensuring my gloves could not possibly be any whiter without being eaten by bleach. This was my chance to say thank you and goodbye to someone I had never met but owed so much.

Although proud and honored to be a part of LCDR Hartman's funeral, I was extremely nervous that morning. It's not every day you get to honor a figure of women's history or participate in her final chapter.

The air was brisk and clean, but the day snowy and very gray. But as I stood by the van, anxiously awaiting my cue from the funeral director, I had never seen my uniform put off such a shine and glow.

As family, friends and guests took their seats and places underneath the tent near the flag-draped coffin, I struggled to keep back tears. I had seen this sight before, too many times to count, but today was different. Thoughts of this woman's achievements and what her duty meant to me as a fellow servicewoman were overwhelming.

It became silent in the tent, and then the preacher started to talk. About ten minutes later the funeral director gave me a cue, and in Honor Guard fashion I started my slow march to the tent.

The flag was then folded and in my hands. At that moment, I realized the flag itself is not just a parting gift. It stands for something so much more.

Not only do the colors symbolize the United States of America, but each thread woven into its fabric represents everyone who has ever served, or is now serving. Just as I am a thread within the flag, so is LCDR Hartman due to her devotion to duty and country, and her dedication and sacrifice for protecting the homeland.

With flag in hand, I made a left face and took three steps to stand in front of her daughter. Bent at the waist and holding the flag in front of me, I said, "On behalf of the President of the United States, United States Coast Guard and a grateful nation . . ." I could barely hear myself speak over the sound of my heart pounding in my ears.

I finished speaking and handed the flag to her daughter. Then I straightened up and saluted the flag her daughter now held. At that moment, I was the proudest, saddest and happiest I have ever been at once.

At the end of my salute I slowly exited the tent. The funeral had concluded so I made my way back to the van, where I found an older woman in a fur coat waiting for me. She introduced herself as Betty, and told me how grateful she was for my presence at her friend's funeral, and said that she, too, had been a SPAR.

We talked for a bit and I don't know who was more excited – me, for the opportunity of getting to speak with her, or her, for getting to speak to a young woman in today's Coast Guard.

I gave her a hug – despite the fact I still wore my uniform – and then started putting my things in the van.

When I was ready to leave Betty gave me a necklace, a gold chain with the Women's Memorial Coin attached as a pendant. I still have it to this day, and every time I look at it I think of Betty and LCDR Hartman.

I would encourage all women in today's military to take the opportunity to speak with older servicewomen and veterans, who have such memorable stories, and to thank them for opening the way.

Marine Science Technician Third Class Jayne Anne Tragesser
U.S. Coast Guard

*"Old soldiers never die; they just fade away."*
General Douglas MacArthur

# AFTERWORD

*"In war there is no second prize for the runner-up."*
General Omar N. Bradley

Dozens of military experiences have been shared in this collection, as anecdotes or motivational bios. Each of the women showcased has presented a colorful glimpse of life in uniform, and every account is unique.

Interestingly, some of these women are related or closely connected through military contact. But due to the vast number of variables such as time, place and type of training, mentors and friends, and even world conditions, the military experience is different from one soldier, coastie, sailor, airman, or marine to the next.

Life is a plethora of emotions and opportunities that vary greatly in degree and point of view. Seldom are these moments identical, and even more rarely are they interpreted or recounted similarly.

With so many of our young men and women donning their uniform of choice and stepping into their boots with eyes wide open, even the competition between the branches of Army, Navy, Air Force, Coast Guard and Marine Corps is healthy and ongoing.

Amid all these differences and varying factors, however, one component remains steadfast and unyielding: The patriotism of the American soldier.

Ultimately all servicemen and women are prepared to sacrifice everything for our great nation. And "all of them," as Kira Johnson states most eloquently in her story, "are doing the same job, for the same country, and for similar reasons."

Michele Hunter Mirabile

*"People sleep peaceably in their beds at night only because rough men stand ready to do violence on their behalf."*

George Orwell

Made in the USA